THE BOOK
OF
CHRISTMAS

THE BOOK
OF
CHRISTMAS

STORIES, POEMS, AND RECIPES FOR SHARING THAT MOST WONDERFUL TIME OF YEAR

Jessica Faust AND Jacky Sach

CITADEL PRESS
Kensington Publishing Corp.
www.kensingtonbooks.com

CITADEL PRESS BOOKS are published by

Kensington Publishing Corp.
850 Third Avenue
New York, NY 10022

First printing: October 2002

10 9 8 7 6 5 4 3 2 1

Printed in the United States of America

Text design by Stanley S. Drate / Folio Graphics Co. Inc.

Library of Congress Control Number: 2002104521

ISBN: 0-8065-2368-9

May the spirit of Christmas
be with you all year 'round . . .

Contents

Acknowledgments

It was such a thrill putting this book together. Since both of us love Christmas, it was a joy not only to share our own ideas and traditions, but to hear what others do as well. And thankfully there were so many people who were willing to share those with us. For all the help they have given us, we would like to thank the following people.

We would both like to thank:

Our editor Bob Shuman, not only for being a terrific person, but for giving us the chance to do this book.

Aimee Schnabel, Kim DeRoche, Kris Curry, Carol Kortus, June Sach, Nicky Westcott, Terri Fernandez, Jim and Elaine Flynn, Linda Faust, Rose Carroll, Lila Faust, Maurine Peterson, Nancy Kynaston, Judy Keever, and Laura Mahnke, for contributing so many wonderful family recipes and craft or holiday ideas.

Jessica would like to thank:

All of her family and friends for making every Christmas and every day special.

And a special dedication to Grandpa Bob (Santa), the ultimate Christmas Elf. Never does a year go by when we don't miss you dearly.

Jacky would like to thank:

Her family, who always make Christmas the best day of the year. Especially Dad, who taught her patience and the agony of anticipation by always making the family wait until after breakfast to open their presents.

With a special thanks to Mom, who taught her the importance of the little things and the joy in giving to others.

And of course, Roscoe, who always manages to knock over the Christmas tree.

THE BOOK
OF
CHRISTMAS

1

A Christmas Story

What is Christmas?
It is tenderness for the past, courage for the present,
hope for the future. It is a fervent wish that every
cup may overflow with blessings rich and eternal,
and that every path may lead to peace.

—Agnes M. Pharo

*W*hile the most important story of Christmas is the birth of Jesus—after all, this is why we celebrate the holiday—there are many stories as to why Christmas is celebrated as it is today. In this chapter we'll start with the birth of Jesus, but also take a look at how the many traditions we now have came to be—such as Christmas trees, Santa Claus, and hanging stockings.

The Christmas Story

There is no better way to tell the story of how Christmas began than to use the words that first brought it to our attention, those of Luke from the Holy Bible. So gather together friends and family and read aloud this terrific story of how Christmas came to be.

From Luke 2: 1–20

2:1
And it came to pass in those days, that there went out a decree from Caesar Augustus that all the world should be taxed.

2:2
(And this taxing was first made when Cyrenius was governor of Syria.)

2:3
And all went to be taxed, every one into his own city.

2:4
And Joseph also went up from Galilee, out of the city of Nazareth, into Judaea, unto the city of David, which is called Bethlehem; (because he was of the house and lineage of David:)

2:5
To be taxed with Mary his espoused wife, being great with child.

2:6
And so it was, that, while they were there, the days were accomplished that she should be delivered.

2:7
And she brought forth her firstborn son, and wrapped him in swaddling clothes, and laid him in a manger; because there was no room for them in the inn.

2:8
And there were in the same country shepherds abiding in the field, keeping watch over their flock by night.

2:9
And, lo, the angel of the Lord came upon them, and the glory of the Lord shone round about them: and they were sore afraid.

2:10
And the angel said unto them, Fear not: for, behold, I bring you good tidings of great joy, which shall be to all people.

2:11
For unto you is born this day in the city of David a Saviour, which is Christ the Lord.

2:12
And this shall be a sign unto you; Ye shall find the babe wrapped in swaddling clothes, lying in a manger.

2:13
And suddenly there was with the angel a multitude of the heavenly host praising God, and saying,

2:14
Glory to God in the highest, and on earth peace, good will toward men.

2:15
And it came to pass, as the angels were gone away from them into heaven, the shepherds said one to another, Let us now go even unto Bethlehem, and see this thing which is come to pass, which the Lord hath made known unto us.

2:16
And they came with haste, and found Mary, and Joseph, and the babe lying in a manger.

2:17
And when they had seen it, they made known abroad the saying which was told them concerning this child.

2:18
And all they that heard it wondered at those things which were told them by the shepherds.

2:19
But Mary kept all these things, and pondered them in her heart.

2:20
And the shepherds returned, glorifying and praising God for all the things that they had heard and seen, as it was told unto them.

Christmas Celebrations

While the celebration of Christmas is fairly new (at least in all of human history), the celebration of a midwinter festival dates back to prehistoric times. During early history, the festival was a celebration of the beginning of longer days (or more daylight), and people gathered together to feast and thank the gods. Surprisingly, many of our Christmas traditions can still be traced back to these early celebrations.

It wasn't until the fourth century, around A.D. 340, that Christmas was declared an official holiday. It was during this time the Christian Roman Emperor Constantine established Christmas and decided that December 25 would be the official day of celebration. His choice of December 25 was not because it was the birthday of Christ. Instead, Constantine chose that day because it was already a day of celebration in the Roman Empire. It was the Feast of Saturn, a pagan holiday celebrated with a two-week period of feasting, drinking, music, no work, and the exchange of gifts. Since Constantine was the first Christian emperor of the Roman Empire it was his desire to eliminate these pagan rituals and Christianize his people. While Constantine was obviously successful, there are a surprising number of traditions still practiced that originate from those pagan ceremonies.

The first, and one of the universal Christmas traditions, is gift giving. This custom can be traced back to the Feast of Saturn or Saturnalia. The first gifts were simple things such as good luck charms, food, and eventually small items such as jewelry, candles, and statues of gods. When Christmas became a Church-recognized holiday, gift giving was viewed as a pagan tradition and severely frowned upon. However, tradition prevailed over Church sentiment and soon the exchange of gifts was justified by the original gift giving of the Magi, and from figures such as St. Nicholas.

Over hundreds of years, St. Nicholas has taken many forms and many names, but his overall sentiment is the same. He is the wonderful white-haired hero of adults and children alike, delivering gifts, hopes, and dreams around the world. In America he is known as Santa Claus, in Britain Father Christmas, and in Germany he's Kris Kringle. Whatever you call this bearer of gifts, all cultures have one thing in common—this hero of Christmas legends is based upon a real-live hero, St. Nicholas.

Orphaned at an early age, St. Nicholas lived in Turkey around A.D. 300. At seventeen, he became one of the youngest priests ever and used the wealth he had inherited from his family to give gifts to the needy, especially children. Legends tell of him dropping bags of gold down chimneys or throwing them into windows, where the gifts landed in stockings hung by the fireplace to dry. It is said that St. Nicholas actually had a white beard and wore a long flowing red cape, hence the image of our modern-day Santa.

The American version of Santa Claus actually comes from the Dutch Sinterklaas. Stories of his climbing down chimneys on Christmas Eve to leave toys all come from Dutch traditions. However, it wasn't until the nineteenth century that Santa became characterized by his bright red suit with white fur trim. In 1822, American minister Clement C. Moore's famous poem *A Visit from Saint Nicholas* inspired Thomas Nast to draw Santa, giving us a definite way to look at the guy in red.

It's amazing to know that not only are many of our Christmas customs universal, but so are many of our decorations. Hanging wreaths by the door or using greenery to decorate mantels, banisters, and railings occurs throughout the world. The custom originated during the Roman celebrations as an exchange to honor the god Saturn. In early English tradition, wreaths were placed outside doors to keep away evil spirits. Decorating a tree actually comes from Germany and, although celebrated throughout the world, is not as universal as many other traditions. The tradition originally spread outside Germany when Prince Apoundert of Germany married Queen Victoria of England and set up a splendid tree in Windsor Castle.

He had servants trim the tree with candies, sugared fruits, and tiny wrapped gifts.

✳

One of the most beloved symbols of Christmas is the Nativity scene, a tradition that originated in Italy with St. Francis of Assisi. St. Francis created a manger scene and performed mass in front of it, inspiring awe and devotion in all who attended.

Christmas Around the World

The United States of America

A celebrated holiday for centuries, Christmas wasn't declared a federal holiday in America until June 26, 1870, by President Ulysses S. Grant.

Today Christmas is celebrated with fervor throughout the United States. While most traditions are similar, a mix of the many cultures that make the United States what it is, there are also many differences dependent on the region of the country you live in.

In California and Florida, you'll see palm trees emblazoned with lights, while the Rocky Mountain states often celebrate with decorated pine trees in the snow. The Southwest is known for their chili pepper wreaths and Maine for their great evergreens. Wherever you go, however, it is hard to miss the commonality among different cultures coming together for a single celebration.

Austria

Christmas in Austria actually begins on December 6, the day of St. Nicholas. This is when the legendary gift-giver makes his rounds. Dressed in a shimmering robe and accompanied by Knecht Rupnecht, his impish assistant, St. Nicholas can be seen in the streets bestowing sweets and apples on good children while his companion playfully calls the bad children to feel the punishing lash of his whip.

Much like Christmas Eve in America, December 24 in Austria is often filled with last-minute shopping and preparation. In the countryside, farmers inscribe the initials of the Three Wise Men on the archway of stable doors—C for Caspar, M for Melchoir, and B for Balthazar. The chalking is believed to act as a talisman, protecting the herd from sickness in the coming year. On Christmas Eve the trees are lit and in many villages people dressed as "shelter seekers" trudge through snow, going from farm to farm in a reenactment of the plight of Mary and Joseph as they sought shelter on the eve of Christ's birth.

After church, families return home for Christmas Eve dinner, a meal traditionally consisting of braised carp, served with a hearty and aromatic gingerbread and beer sauce, and *topfen-palatschinken*, sweet cheese crêpes baked into a smooth and creamy custard and slathered with a blissful apricot caramel sauce.

In Austria gifts are brought by Kristkindl, a golden-haired baby with wings who symbolizes the newborn Christ.

Belgium

Much like Austria, Christmas in Belgium begins on December 6 with the arrival of St. Nicholas. Dressed in robes, St. Nicholas rides on a white horse and leaves gifts in the shoes children set out by the fireplace. The children leave vegetables by the fireplace for St. Nicholas's horse.

Most of the Christmas celebration is left until December 25. It is on this day that a traditional Belgium meal of *speculoos*—spiced cookies—and *aardappel kroketjes*—fried potato croquettes—are served. After dinner has been eaten and the table cleaned up, you'll see groups of Belgians flock to the frounceen canals for an afternoon of skating.

Often while people are skating or eating, three men, chosen to portray the three kings, move from house to house singing carols.

England

When you look at England's Christmas traditions, it is easy to see where many of the customs of the United States come from, including Christmas cards, decorations, and even caroling.

Christmas Day in England is celebrated by opening presents left by Father Christmas and attending church services. Christmas dinner traditionally consists of roast turkey or goose with stuffing, Yorkshire pudding, and roast potatoes. This is followed by mince pies and Christmas pudding flaming with brandy, which might contain hidden coins or charms for the children. Traditionally, the pudding is prepared weeks beforehand, with each family member stirring the pudding while making a wish. Later in the day many families will serve Christmas cake—a rich fruit cake with marzipan, icing, and sugar frosting.

Invented by a London baker in 1846, Christmas crackers often accompany meals at Christmas. A cracker is a brightly colored paper tube twisted and tied with a ribbon at both ends. When pulled, the cracker pops open to reveal a party hat like a crown, a fortune or riddle, or a small toy or other trinket (such as a plastic ring). Recently, Christmas crackers have shown up with increasing frequency in American gift shops, suggesting the tradition has emigrated to the United States.

Boxing Day, or the day after Christmas, is just as important to England as Christmas. There are a few different theories on how Boxing Day originated.

Some say Boxing Day originated with the practice of giving cash or durable goods to those less fortunate—the lower classes who were busy taking care of the higher ups on Christmas day. Others say it was the practice of giving tradespeople—people who called regularly during the year, such as the milkman— monetary tips or food items. Yet another legend is that Boxing Day started the tradition of opening the alms boxes placed in churches during the Christmas season. The contents of the alms boxes were then distributed amongst the poor of the parish. Whatever the original meaning of Boxing Day, the holiday's roots can be traced to Britain, where this holiday is also known as St. Stephen's Day. It is also celebrated in Australia, New

Zealand, and Canada. Today, the holiday has evolved into an extension of Christmas. It's another day to spend with the family and have a wonderful English roast dinner, while watching English football or having some family fun.

Ethiopia

Ganna, the Ethiopian Christmas, is traditionally celebrated January 7. Ethiopians begin the holiday by attending church. Afterward, dinner includes *injera*—a sourdough pancake-like bread—and *doro wat*—a spicy chicken stew.

Gift giving is a very small part of Christmas in Ethiopia.

France

Christmas celebrations begin in France on Christmas Eve, when children place their shoes in front of the fireplace hoping that Père Noël will fill them with gifts. It is also traditional to attend a midnight church service followed by *le reveillon*, a meal that represents Christ's birth. The meal often consists of the *bûche de Noël*—cake rolled and filled with chestnut cream then coated in homemade marzipan. Families used to have a Three Kings Cake with a treat hidden in it. Whoever found the treat got to be king—or queen—for the day.

After the festivities, it is customary to leave a candle burning, just in case the Virgin Mary passes that way.

Germany

Legends say that for the pure of heart in Germany on Christmas Eve, rivers turn to wine, animals speak to each other, tree blossoms bear fruit, mountains open up to reveal precious gems, and church bells can be heard ringing from the bottom of the sea. Since few are actually pure of heart enough to witness such miracles, the rest must content themselves by beginning Christmas celebrations on December 6, St. Nicholas Day.

During the night of December 6, St. Nicholas hops from house to house leaving gifts in the shoes of good children and filling those of bad children with twigs.

However, this is all just a prelude to the real Christmas excitement, Christmas Eve and the presentation of the Christmas tree, a tradition that originated in Germany. Since the tree is kept a secret until this unveiling, it is an especially big event. A room is locked before Christmas. On Christmas Eve the children are woken up at midnight and taken to the locked room, which has secreted the lit Christmas tree and presents. When the family enters the room, carols are sung, the Christmas story is read, and gifts are opened.

Christmas Day dinner traditionally consists of roast goose, *christstollen* (long loaves of bread with nuts, raisins, citron, and dried fruit), *lebkuchen* (spice bars), marzipan, and *Dresden stollen* (a moist, heavy bread filled with fruit).

Greece

In Greece, gifts are exchanged on January 1, St. Basil's Day. The Greek Orthodox religion states that Santa Claus is in fact St. Basil. St. Basil's love for children, the unprotected, and the poor gave him this standing in Greek culture. On this day, children receive gifts and a silver coin is baked into a sponge-like New Year's cake called *vasilopeta*. When serving the dish, the first slice is set aside for St. Basil and the second slice for Christ. The following slices go to members of the family in descending order of age. Whoever gets the coin gets all the luck!

Holland

While many of the Christmas traditions celebrated in the United States originally came from Holland, there are still a number that did not. For instance, St Nicholas first arrives in Holland from Spain in the month of November. Dressed in robes, he travels by boat with Black Peter, his assistant. When he arrives, crowds throng the docks in Amsterdam to greet St. Nicholas and watch him ride his snow horse through the streets. It is said that for most of the year St. Nicholas prepares lists and presents for all the children, noting if they are good or bad.

It isn't until December 5, however, Sinterklaas Eve, that children can finally see some of the fruits of St. Nicholas's labor.

It is on this day that presents are given and received. Christmas Day is spent feasting on *oliebollen*—or oil balls—bite-size flour and raisin pastries that are deep-fried and sprinkled with sugar.

Ireland

To the Irish, Christmas is still very much a religious holiday. On Christmas Eve, many visitors will be surprised to see the number of lighted red candles placed in windows. These candles are meant as a guide for Joseph and Mary as they look for shelter.

In preparation for the holidays, the Irish traditionally bake a seed cake for each person in the house. They also make three puddings, one for Christmas, one for New Year's Day, and one for the Twelfth Night. The true meal, however, is a Christmas morning feast of eggs, bacon, grilled tomatoes, mushrooms, potatoes, sausages, fried bread, and links of black and white pudding. Then, as if that weren't enough food, the midday meal includes everything from roast ham to potato-stuffed turkey and spiced beef.

After the Christmas evening meal, bread and milk are left out and the door is left unlocked as a symbol of hospitality.

Italy

Christmas Eve in Italy is a time for viewing Italy's great number of artistic and elaborate manger scenes. Using the traditional scene with Joseph, Mary, Baby Jesus, and the animals, artists use their imaginations to create intricate landscapes. They might include grottoes, small trees, lakes, rivers, the lights of Bethlehem in the background, angels hung from wires, and occasionally, even local heroes. Often, towns will have contests among churches for the best display. Christmas Eve is also a time of feasting.

Amid the Christmas Eve celebrations, Christmas candles are lighted and a Christmas banquet is spread. In some places, Christmas Eve dinner consists largely of fish. Another popular dish besides the *panettone*, a cake filled with candied fruit, of course, is *cotechino*, a fresh pork sausage traditionally served with stewed lentils. As a rule, most Christmas sweets in Italy will contain nuts like almonds. Folklore says that eating nuts helps with the fertility of the earth and aids in the growth of flocks and family.

Before going to bed on Christmas Eve, children will set out their shoes for the female Santa Claus, La Befana, to fill with gifts. At noon on Christmas day, the pope bestows his blessings on the crowds amassed in Vatican Square.

Mexico

Christmas celebrations in Mexico begin on December 16, the first night of Las Posadas, which last until December 24 and commemorate the journey of Mary and Joseph from Nazareth to Bethlehem.

Each night during this time, the celebrants carry images of Joseph and Mary, looking for shelter through the streets. Members of the company, all with lighted candles, sing the *Litany of the Virgin* as they approach the door of the house assigned to the first Posada. Together they wake members of the house to ask for lodging for Mary. The members of the household refuse and the celebrants move on. The visits continue until an owner of a house throws open the doors and bids them welcome.

When the Posada procession at last finds a home it's time for the piñata, food, and dancing. A piñata is usually a colorfully painted paper container filled with candy and toys. It is hung from the ceiling or a tree, and one by one, the children are blindfolded, turned around, and instructed to strike the piñata with a stick. When the piñata is broken, there is an explosion of goodies for everyone.

On midnight on Christmas Eve, the birth of Christ is celebrated with fireworks, ringing bells, and blowing whistles. After attending mass, families return home for a traditional dinner that often includes tamales, rice, rellenos, and atole, a sweet traditional drink. Santa Claus does not play a big role in a Mexican Christmas celebration, but his suit color is reflected in the beautiful poinsettia. Legend has it that a poor boy went to visit the nativity scene at church with only some green branches as an offering. The townsfolk laughed at him but once he placed the greenery at the scene the red flowers of the poinsettia bloomed on each branch.

Poland

Christmas Eve in Poland officially begins on the sighting of the first star. Poles view this little star, or Gwiazdka, in remembrance of the star of Bethlehem. On Christmas Eve people anxiously gather together to watch the sky, hoping to be the first to see it. The moment the star appears, greetings and good wishes are exchanged. Then families head inside for the most important meal of the year, Christmas supper. The table is set to perfection with bits of hay underneath the tablecloth as a reminder that Christ was born in a manger. Tradition also states that you must have an even number of people seated around the table or someone might die in the coming year.

Each year, Christmas dinner begins with the breaking of the *Oplatek*, a semitransparent wafer of unleavened dough stamped with scenes of the nativity. The wafer is passed around the table and everyone breaks off a piece and eats it as a symbol of their unity with Christ. Custom also prescribes that the number of dishes in the meal be odd, nine or eleven. An even number would eliminate any hope of newfound wealth, additional children, or good fortune. Food usually includes poppy seed cake, borscht (beet soup), prune dumplings, and noodles with poppy seeds.

Once dinner is finished, the guests often sit around the Christmas tree telling stories and singing songs. Sometimes the Christmas trees are left as they are until the feast of St. Mary of the Candle Lighting, on February 2.

Portugal

Instead of a Christmas tree, Portugese families often gather around a nativity crèche to celebrate the holiday.

Christmas breakfast is a feast known as the *consoda*. Families set extra places at the breakfast table for the souls of the departed, hoping these souls will therefore bestow upon them good fortune in the coming year. Christmas dinner in Portugal is celebrated with a dish of dried codfish, called *bacalhau*, with a dessert of *rabanadas*, slices of white bread soaked in eggs and wine, dredged in sugar, and fried until the coating is crusty and candylike.

Children place their shoes by the fireplace in the hopes that Baby Jesus, instead of Santa, will leave them a piece of Bolo Rei, a circular cake coated in glazed fruits, crushed nuts, and sugar icing.

Spain

Celebrations in Spain begin with Hogueras (bonfires), a tradition that originated long before Christmas itself. Hogueras is the observance of the winter solstice, the shortest day of the year and the beginning of winter.

Christmas dinner is eaten on Christmas Eve, but never until after midnight. It is a family feast, and often highlighted by Pavo Trufado de Navidad (Christmas turkey with truffles). After the meal, family members gather around the Christmas tree and sing Christmas carols and hymns of Christendom. The rejoicing continues through the wee hours of the morning.

Unlike the tradition of most countries that celebrate Christmas, Spanish children must wait until January 6 for the delivery of their presents. On the Eve of Epiphany, January 5, children place their shoes on the doorstep and await the Three Wise Men. Legend says that the Three Wise Men traveled through Spain on their way to Bethlehem.

Sweden

Christmas celebrations in Sweden begin on December 13 with Lucia Day. Legend says that December 13 is the longest night of the year, a night when everyone and everything needs extra nourishment. A Lucia (Queen of Light)—usually the youngest daughter—is chosen from each home and dressed in a white gown with a red sash and a crown of candles in her hair. Accompanied by her white-clad attendants, she brings coffee, rolls, ginger biscuits, and glogg (a mulled wine) to the rest of the family. The custom dates back to the fourth century when a Christian virgin named Lucia was martyred for her beliefs.

Christmas Eve is the primary holiday celebration in Sweden. On this day no work is to be done except for last-minute preparations of the splendid Christmas smorgasbord, or meal. Dishes such as ham, jellied pigs feet, lutfisk—cod fish soaked in lye—and rice porridge are traditional.

After Christmas dinner has been cleared away, Swedish children await the arrival of the Tomte, the Christmas elf who lives under floorboards and looks after the family and livestock and brings presents at Christmas.

Christmas trees are usually brought home and decorated two days before Christmas.

Vietnam

The historic Vietnamese religions are Buddhism, Taoism, and Confucianism. However, during French rule many people became Christians, and Christmas is therefore celebrated.

After midnight church services on Christmas Eve, Vietnamese Christians return to their homes for a dinner consisting of chicken soup, and much like European custom, children will leave their shoes out in the hopes that they made Father Christmas's good list.

It seems the world over people celebrate Christmas with gusto. It's a beautiful holiday with wonderful traditions from East to West and in between!

2

Prayers and Songs of Christmas

Strike the harp and join the chorus.
—From the Christmas carol "Deck the Halls"

*I*magine a Christmas without prayers, hymns, or carols. It's hard to do. Whether you're singing "Jingle Bells" while finishing your shopping, or "Away in a Manger" during midnight mass, Christmas carols and prayers are as much a part of Christmas as Christmas trees and Santa Claus.

Many people have a favorite prayer they say before Christmas dinner, and others like to gather around the piano and share.

Prayers

Prayer for the Nativity

O God,
whose mighty Son was born in Bethlehem
those days long ago,
lead us to that same poor place,
where Mary laid her tiny Child.
And as we look on in wonder and praise,
make us welcome him in all new life,
see him in the poor,
and care for his handiwork
the earth, the sky and the sea.
O God, bless us again in your great love.
We pray for this through Christ our Lord.
Amen.

Prayer Around the Christmas Tree

Lord
our God,
the heavens are
the work of your hands,
the moon and the stars you
made;
the earth and the sea, and every
living creature came into being
by your word. And all of us, too.
May this tree bring cheer to this house
through Jesus Christ your good and holy Son,
who brings life
and beauty to us
and to our world.
Lighting this tree, we hope in His promise.

Christmas Novena

Let Us Pray . . .
Hail and blessed be the hour and moment
in which the Son of God was born of the most pure Virgin
Mary,
at midnight,
in Bethlehem, in piercing cold.
In that hour vouchsafe,
O my God,
to hear my prayer and grant my desires,
through the merits of Our Savior Jesus Christ,
and of His Blessed Mother.
Amen.

Christmas Prayer

Christ born in a stable is born in me
Christ accepted by shepherds accepts me
Christ receiving the wise men receives me
Christ revealed to the nations be revealed in me
Christ dwelling in Nazareth You dwell in me
Christ, grant that people may look at me and see Your Presence.
Amen.

Dinner Prayer

Leader: Lord Jesus,
in the peace of this season our spirits are joyful:
With the beasts and angels,
the shepherds and stars,
with Mary and Joseph we sing God's praise.
By your coming may the hungry be filled with good things,
and may our table and home be blessed.

Together: Bless us O Lord, and these Thy gifts,
which we are about to receive from Thy bounty
through Christ our Lord. Amen.

Breakfast Prayer

The Word was made flesh, alleluia, alleluia!
And dwelt among us, alleluia, alleluia!

Let the heavens rejoice and the earth be glad, before the face of
the Lord, for He comes.
Bless us, O Lord, and these Thy gifts, which we are about to
receive from Thy bounty.
Through Christ our Lord. Amen.

Breakfast Prayer

Glory to God in the highest, and on earth peace to men of good
will, alleluia! The Lord has reigned, and He is clothed with
beauty. Almighty God, the Savior of the world, who hast nour-
ished us with heavenly food, we give Thee thanks for the gift
of this bodily refreshment which we have received from Thy
bountiful mercy. Through Christ our Lord. Amen.

If you want to add a little music to your Christmas celebration why not consider getting the music and lyrics for some of
these great classic cards and sing them on your own?

- Away in a Manger
- Deck the Halls
- God Rest You Merry Gentlemen
- Hark! The Herald Angels Sing
- Jingle Bells
- O Christmas Tree
- O Little Town of Bethlehem
- Silent Night
- We Wish You a Merry Christmas
- We Three Kings of Orient Are
- Do You Hear What I Hear?
- The First Nöel
- Must Be Santa
- Carol of the Bells
- Here Comes Santa Claus

- Rudolph the Red-Nosed Reindeer
- O Come, All Ye Faithful
- Good King Wenceslas
- Joy to the World
- Little Drummer Boy
- The Christmas Song
- I'll Be Home for Christmas
- I Saw Mommy Kissing Santa Claus
- Jingle Bell Rock
- The Twelve Days of Chritmas
- All I Want for Christmas Is My Two Front Teeth
- Here We Come A-Wassailing
- The Holly and the Ivy
- It Came Upon a Midnight Clear

Family Favorites

Everyone has prayers and blessings that are traditionally used on Christmas. Write down your family favorites here.

TITLE _____

_____

_____

_____

_____

_____

_____

_____

_____

_____

_____

_____

_____

❧

TITLE _____

_____

_____

_____

_____

_____

_____

_____

_____

_____

_____

_____

_____

TITLE _____

_____
_____
_____
_____
_____
_____
_____
_____
_____
_____
_____
_____
_____
_____
_____
_____

❈

TITLE _____

_____
_____
_____
_____
_____
_____
_____
_____
_____
_____
_____
_____
_____
_____

❈

3

The Christmas Feast

One cannot think well, love well,
sleep well, if one has not dined well.
—Virginia Woolf

Christmas is celebrated all over the world, and Christmas in America is one holiday that really shows what a melting pot this country is. In the following collection of recipes, you'll get a taste for what Christmas is like all over this great country of ours. You'll see traditional favorites originating from Louisiana, England, Sweden, and Minnesota, and learn what it is like to cele-brate Christmas in Boston, Los Angeles, and New York.

Whether you choose recipes from those passed along from our family and friends, or add your own family favorites in the space provided, we'll guarantee you'll find something that will please the entire family for years to come.

BEVERAGES

Whether you're looking for a delicious drink to start or end your meal, or something warm for a cold winter day, these wintery, Christmasy beverages are pleasing for old and young. They can be a special part of your holiday celebrations or a warm offering for cold sledders and skaters.

Brandy Milk Punch

A delicious recipe from Aimee Schnabel that can be varied with your eggnog, but we warn you: This recipe is not for the calorie counter!

SERVES 50. CAN BE HALVED.

- 2 pounds sugar
- 1–2 cups boiling water
- 10 quarts half-and-half (or 5 quarts half-and-half and 5 quarts milk)
- 1 fifth of brandy (We recommend Christian Brothers.)
- 3 ounces vanilla extract
- 1 1/2 gallons vanilla ice cream
- 1/2 ounce nutmeg

Dissolve sugar in water. Let cool. Combine with half–and–half, brandy, and vanilla. May be stored now. When ready to serve, scoop ice cream into bowl and pour punch on top. Serve sprinkled with nutmeg.

Elegant Eggnog

Spice up your eggnog with this recipe from the files of Jessica's Great-Aunt Maurine Peterson.

SERVES 25.

    1 quart dairy eggnog
    1 quart vanilla ice cream
    2 28-ounce bottles 7-Up
    nutmeg

Combine eggnog and softened ice cream in punch bowl. Slowly add chilled 7-Up. Dust lightly with nutmeg. For extra pizzazz, spice with bourbon, brandy, or Kahlua.

Chocolate Eggnog

A wonderful variation on the traditional Christmas drink.

MAKES 7 $^{1}/_{2}$-CUP SERVINGS.

    1 cup prepared eggnog
    $^{1}/_{3}$ cup chocolate syrup
    1 cup whipping cream
    2 tbs sugar
    2 tbs cocoa

Blend eggnog with chocolate syrup and chill. When chilled, whip cream with sugar and cocoa and fold into the eggnog. Serve with a little bit of cocoa powder sprinkled on top.

Glogg

🌟

An essential drink at any Swedish Christmas—for adults only!

MAKES 16 SERVINGS.

3 whole cardamom seeds
3 whole cloves
1 cinnamon stick
1 strip of orange rind (about 4 inches)—orange part only
1¹/₃ cups water
¹/₃ cup blanched almonds
¹/₂ cup golden raisins
1 bottle dry red wine
1 bottle port wine
¹/₂ bottle cognac
sugar to taste

Tie cardamom, cloves, cinnamon, and orange rind together in a cheesecloth bag. Or place in a mulling spice strainer if you have one. Place in water and bring to a boil. Simmer covered for about 10 minutes.

Add almonds and raisins and simmer for 10 more minutes. Add wine, port, and cognac and bring to a quick boil.

Remove from heat. Cool and store, covered, overnight.

At serving time remove the spice bag and heat glogg to a slight simmer—just warm enough to drink, but not boiling. Add sugar to taste.

Serve with almonds and raisins in each glass.

Mulled Cider

Let the wonderful aromas fill the house with the delicious scent of Christmas!

MAKES 10 SERVINGS.

- 1 tsp whole allspice
- 1 tsp whole cloves
- dash of nutmeg
- 3 3-inch cinnamon sticks
- ⅓ cup sugar
- 2 quarts apple cider (pasteurized)
- 1 orange, sliced

Place spices into a mulling spice ball or wrap in cheesecloth and tie with string. Place spice ball into a pan with cider and orange slices and simmer for about 20 minutes. Strain spices after you simmer.

For a delicious twist on this Christmas favorite add a splash of Captain Morgan Spiced Rum or replace the cider with red wine.

APPETIZERS

Every meal, particularly on special occasions, should start with delicious appetizers. These dinner openers are a great way to welcome guests as they walk in the door and an even better way to soothe hungry tummies while waiting for the main event. Vegetarians and meat eaters will love the selection included in this short, but yummy list.

Nicky's Chicken Liver Pâté

No English Christmas meal is complete without this delicious starter, from Jacky's aunt Nicky.

  1 large onion
  3 garlic cloves
  butter for frying and topping
  1 pound bacon
  1 pound chicken livers
  1 pound pig's liver
  1 ounce brandy

Sauté onions and garlic in butter until transparent. Remove from the pan and add bacon, cooking slowly. Add livers and more butter as needed. Remove from heat and allow to cool. Add brandy and pass the mixture through a Cuisinart. Turn pâté into buttered dishes and drizzle melted butter on top of each.

  (This recipe is very rich! You can always freeze in small containers and use as needed.)

Faux Liver Pâté

For the vegetarian liver lovers, from the recipe files of June Sach.

- 1 cup lentils, cooked and drained
- 1 cup walnuts, chopped fine
- 3 hard-boiled eggs, chopped
- 1 huge onion, diced and sautéed
- salt and pepper to taste

To try this veggie alternative to chicken livers, mix all ingredients together and chill—you'll be amazed! It can be frozen, too.

Crabmeat Dip

From the recipe files of June Sach. Yummy!

- 8-ounce package cream cheese
- 1 tsp milk
- 8-ounce crabmeat (frozen is best but can use canned)
- 1 tbsp chopped onion
- 1/2 tsp horseradish
- 1/2 tsp lemon juice

Preheat oven to 375 degrees F.

Soften cream cheese by adding milk and mixing together. Add remaining ingredients. Mix together until well blended.

Grease ovenproof dish and bake for 15 minutes or until hot and bubbly.

Serve with crackers or rye bread rounds.

Holiday Artichoke Dip

Jessica's annual Christmas party would not be complete without this dip. Each year the recipe gets doubled and doubled again, and yet there never seems to be enough.

> 1 can artichoke hearts (not the marinated kind)
> 1 cup mayonnaise (Miracle Whip doesn't work)
> 1 cup grated parmesan cheese
> 2 small cans diced green chilies or 1 fresh jalapeño

Dice the artichoke hearts into small pieces. Mix all ingredients together in small baking dish. Bake at 350 degrees F for about 30 minutes or until bubbly and just beginning to brown.

ARTICHOKE DIP FLORENTINE

Add one 10-ounce package chopped spinach.

CRABBY ARTICHOKE DIP

Omit the chilies and add 8 ounces of crabmeat.

PEPPERY ARTICHOKE DIP

Omit the chilies and add one 7-ounce jar roasted red peppers, diced.

SOUP

There's nothing better on a cold winter day than a warm bowl of delicious homemade soup. Not only do these recipes make great Sunday dinners throughout the winter months, but they can also be used as a starter to your Christmas feast. Or—for those who look forward to a large Christmas dinner, but like to keep their Christmas Eve celebrations small—try serving a pot of one of these soups with warm crusty bread on the side. Follow up with Christmas cookies and you have a meal everyone will love.

Louisiana Oyster and Artichoke Soup

From the kitchen of Dorothy Andrews.

SERVES 6.

2 12-ounce containers fresh standard oysters (or try ³/₄ pound shrimp)

¹/₂ cup finely chopped shallots

1 bay leaf

¹/₈–¹/₄ tsp red pepper

pinch of dried thyme

3 tbsp butter or margarine, melted

3 tbsp all-purpose flour

1 14-ounce can ready-to-serve chicken broth

1 14-ounce can or jar of artichoke hearts, drained and cut into eighths

1 tbsp chopped fresh parsley

¹/₂ tsp salt

¹/₈–¹/₄ tsp hot sauce

3¹/₂ cups whipping cream or half and half

Drain oysters, reserving 1 cup liquid. Cut each oyster into fourths, set aside. Sauté shallots and next four ingredients in butter in a Dutch oven until shallots are tender. Add flour, stirring constantly for 1 minute. Gradually add broth and reserved oyster liquids. Simmer, stirring occasionally, 15 minutes. Remove bay leaf. Add oysters, artichoke hearts, parsley, salt, and hot sauce. Simmer 10 minutes. Stir in whipping cream and cook until thoroughly heated. Don't boil.

Aunt Jenne's Oyster Stew

Aimee Schnabel shares this delicious recipe from Great-Aunt Mary Virginia (Jenne) Potts, on her mother's side of the family, who are from Kosciusko, in the northern part of Mississippi.

SERVES 12.

- butter for sautéing
- Worcestershire sauce
- Tabasco
- onion powder
- chives
- 3 pints oysters
- 2 pints half-and-half
- 2¹/₂ pints whipping cream
- 2 cups milk

In a double boiler, heat 2 inches of butter and the following ingredients to taste: Worcestershire sauce, Tabasco, onion powder, chives (only a little).

Drain oysters and reserve liquid. Cut in quarters.

Add the remaining ingredients, including reserved liquid, saving the oysters for the last few minutes. Heat. Do not boil. You can add 8–10 crumbled saltine crackers, too.

Wild Rice Soup

This soup will fast become a family favorite for any holiday.

MAKES 5 SERVINGS.

- ¹/₂ cup wild rice
- 2¹/₂ cups water
- 2 tbsp butter
- ¹/₂ cup chopped celery
- 1 cup shredded carrots
- ¹/₂ cup chopped onion
- ¹/₂ cup chopped green bell pepper
- 3 tbsp all-purpose flour

1/4 tsp ground black pepper

1 (10³/4-ounce) can vegetable broth

1 cup half-and-half

1/3 cup blanched slivered almonds

1/4 cup fresh parsley

In a small saucepan, combine wild rice with 1¹/2 cups water. Bring to a boil, reduce heat, cover, and simmer for 45 minutes.

In a 3-quart saucepan over medium heat, melt butter; add celery, carrots, onion, and bell pepper. Sauté until vegetables are tender.

Stir in flour, pepper, wild rice, 1 cup water, and broth. Bring to boil and reduce heat. Cover and simmer for 15 minutes.

Stir in half-and-half, almonds, and parsley. Heat until hot and serve.

Fruit Soup

From the Swedish files of Lila Faust. This soup can be eaten as part of your Swedish smorgasbord, for breakfast, or as a dessert.

MAKES 10 SERVINGS.

1 box of prunes

1 cup raisins

1 lemon, sliced (not peeled)

1 orange, sliced (not peeled)

1¹/4 cups sugar

4 tbsp tapioca

1 cinnamon stick

2 apples, diced

Place all the ingredients, except the apples, in a large bowl and cover with water. Soak overnight.

Place in a medium saucepan with the diced apples and cook until just tender. Refrigerate, and serve chilled. The soup can be made up to two days ahead of time.

SALADS

A refreshing way to begin a meal, a small salad will cleanse the palate and ready the stomach for all the good foods to follow. Both fruit and green salads make a terrific addition to a brunch or a yummy snack to eat while opening presents from Santa.

Ambrosia

No Mississippi Christmas meal is served without ambrosia on hand. Sent by Aimee Schnabel.

> 20 navel oranges, peeled and sectioned
> 2 cups shredded coconut
> 1 cup sugar

Combine all ingredients and toss lightly.

Krissy's Christmas Salad

Although Kris doesn't necessarily consider this a salad, we think it's a terrific beginning to any Christmas meal.

> 2 kiwi
> 1 pomegranate

Peel and slice kiwi and pomegranate and arrange beautifully on a platter.

Other terrific fruits to consider for a Christmas fruit salad include:

> star fruit
> blood oranges
> cranberries
> grapefruit
> kumquats
> passion fruit
> papaya

Spinach and Strawberry and Brie Salad
❧

A colorful Christmas salad from the files of Linda Faust.

SERVES 6–8.

 1 package fresh chopped spinach
 2 pints fresh strawberries
 8 ounces Brie cheese

DRESSING:

 ¹/₂ cup sugar
 ¹/₄ cup raspberry vinegar

Place in small pan over low heat, whisking until sugar is dissolved.

ADD:

 2 tbsp poppy seeds
 1 ounce sesame seeds
 ¹/₂ cup oil
 1 tsp paprika
 1 tsp Worcestershire sauce
 1 tsp fine chopped onion

Chill.

MAKES 1 CUP.

Arrange spinach on individual salad plates. Slice strawberries and place on top of spinach then crumble Brie on top. Drizzle with dressing. Add a sprinkling of pine nuts for added flavor if desired.

Apple Beet Salad

Not only is this salad delicious, it's colorful as well!

MAKES 6 SERVINGS.

>   1 (15-ounce) can diced beets
>   2 apples, peeled, cored, and chopped
>   ³/₄ cup chopped walnuts
>   ¹/₂ cup heavy cream, whipped
>   ¹/₄ cup mayonnaise
>   ¹/₂ cup crumbled Gorgonzola or feta cheese

Drain the beets and peel, core, and dice the apples.

In a small bowl, fold together the heavy cream, mayonnaise, and cheese. Set aside.

In a large mixing bowl, combine the beets, apples, walnuts, and cream mixture. Mix together and chill before serving.

ENTRÉES

Whether you eat your Christmas feast for breakfast, lunch, or dinner, these entrées are sure to warm your heart and delight your guests. After all, no meal is complete without an impressive dish to place in the center of your table. Cooking up an easy breakfast casserole or tasty cut of prime rib will not only please your guests, but is sure to garner *oohs* and *aaahs* and, most importantly, leave them begging for more.

Christmas Breakfast Casserole

When celebrating Christmas in Louisiana, Aimee Schnabel says they always start with a special breakfast on Christmas morning. This is from the kitchen of Vicki Petersen Moras, Aimee's Cajun stepmother.

SERVES 6–8.

 12 slices white or wheat bread, cubed
 1½ pounds sausage (links or tube), browned and drained
 1 small can chopped green chilies
 1½ pound grated cheddar cheese
 4 eggs
 2½ cups milk
 1 tbsp mustard
 salt and pepper
 1 can golden mushroom soup
 ¼ cup milk

Place the bread on the bottom of greased 9 × 13-inch dish. Sprinkle the sausage on top of the bread; add a layer of chilies, then grated cheese.

Beat the eggs, milk, mustard, salt, and pepper together; pour over casserole. Cover and refrigerate overnight.

Mix soup with mlk; spread over top. Bake 1½ hours at 300 degrees F, uncovered. Can be frozen.

Pecan Crusted French Toast

For Christmas breakfast or a late-night snack. Amazing!

MAKES 6 SLICES.

> 3 eggs
> 3 tbsp milk
> 1 tsp cinnamon
> 1 tsp nutmeg
> 1/4 cup pecans—finely chopped
> Fresh challah bread
> 2 tbsp butter

In a medium bowl, beat together eggs and milk. Add cinnamon, nutmeg, and chopped pecans.

Slice challah bread into six thick slices.

Heat butter in large skillet. Once butter is heated thoroughly, coat each slice of bread in the egg mixture and place in skillet.

Cook until brown on both sides.

Serve with powdered sugar, fresh fruit, and homemade maple syrup.

Swedish Meatballs

According to Grandma Lila, every Christmas dinner calls for a Swedish smorgasbord of herring, lefse, lingonberries, and, of course, Swedish meatballs.

MAKES 48 MEATBALLS.

> 2 cups bread crumbs (unflavored)
> 1/2 cup milk
> 1 pound ground beef
> 1/4 pound ground veal
> 1/4 pound ground pork
> 1 onion
> 2 tbsp + 1/4 cup butter
> 1 tsp salt

¼ tsp pepper

2 tsp nutmeg

2 tsp paprika

1 tsp dry mustard

3 eggs, beaten

SAUCE

¼ tsp fresh garlic, minced

5 tbsp butter

2 tsp tomato paste

2 cups chicken or beef stock

1 cup sour cream

Preheat oven to 350 degrees F.

Soak the bread crumbs in milk.

Using either your hands or a food processor carefully mix the meat together until it is fully blended. Then mix together the meat and the bread crumbs.

Sauté the onion in 2 tbsp butter until just soft. Mix in salt, pepper, nutmeg, paprika, and mustard. Add to meat mixture along with the eggs. Mix well using your hands. Shape into small meatballs about 1–inch around.

Melt ¼ cup butter in a large skillet over medium heat until just hot. Add meatballs to the butter and brown, being careful not to burn. Remove the meatballs and set them aside.

Sauce: Add garlic and 1 tbsp butter to the fat left in the skillet. Heat until garlic is soft. Blend in the rest of the butter, tomato paste, and stock. Cook over low heat until it thickens slightly.

Pour sauce into a large casserole pan and stir in sour cream. Add meatballs, making sure to cover with sauce.

Bake for 20 to 30 minutes.

Salmon Poached in Orange Sauce

From June and Jacky Sach.

SERVES 6.

2 cups orange juice
1 tsp dried ginger
1 cup marmalade
2 tbsp brown sugar
1 tbsp basalmic vinegar
6 salmon filets

Preheat oven to 350 degrees F.

Mix orange juice, ginger, marmalade, brown sugar, and vinegar together. Heat over low flame until sugar dissolves.

Place salmon filets in a 9 × 11-inch pan and cover with sauce. Cover with aluminum foil.

Bake for half an hour or until fish is cooked all the way through.

Pork Tenderloin

A terrific meal any time of the year.

SERVES 6–8.

4 tbsp flour
salt and pepper to taste
4 pounds pork loin
butter for searing
3 garlic cloves, sliced
1 tsp dried sage

Preheat oven to 325 degrees F.

In a plastic bag, mix the flour and salt and pepper. Add the pork loin and shake until the loin is coated.

Melt butter in a large pan. Add the pork loin and sear (top and bottom).

Remove the pork loin from the heat and place on a cutting

board. Cut 1-inch lengths in the top and stuff with garlic slices. Sprinkle with sage.

Wrap the loin loosely in aluminum foil. Put on a baking sheet or 9×11-inch pan and bake in oven for two hours or until done (if a knife inserted into loin produces blood, keep cooking).

Prime Rib

The perfect celebratory meal.

10 pounds prime rib roast
6 cloves garlic, sliced
salt and ground black pepper to taste
1/2 cup Dijon mustard

Heat oven to 400 degrees F.

Insert slivers of sliced garlic throughout the roast and generously coat with salt, pepper, and mustard.

Place the roast on a rack in a covered roasting pan. Cook for 60 minutes. Then reduce the oven temperature to 325 degrees F, remove the lid, and cook for about 1 hour longer. The thermometer reading of the meat should be between 140 degrees F for rare and 170 degrees F for well done.

When the roast reaches the desired temperature, remove the roasting pan from the oven, place aluminum foil or a lid over the roast, and let it sit for another 30 minutes before slicing.

SIDE DISHES

No meal is complete without a tasty side dish or delicious vegetable concoction. Rather than make the same old green bean casserole (although it is always a wonderful addition to your table) why not try some of these terrific options? Choices for every meal from brunch to dinner, you're sure to find a crowd pleaser in the mix.

Spinach Madeline

From the kitchen of Vicki Petersen Moras.

SERVES 6–8.

4 packages frozen chopped spinach
4 tbsp butter
2 tbsp flour
2 tbsp chopped onion
$^{1}/_{2}$ cup evaporated milk
$^{1}/_{2}$ cup vegetable liquid (from the spinach)
$^{1}/_{2}$ tsp black pepper
$^{3}/_{4}$ tsp celery salt
$^{3}/_{4}$ tsp garlic salt
salt to taste
6 ounces roll of jalapeño cheese or
4 ounces Velveeta and/or cream cheese combined
with a 3-ounce roll of jalapeño or garlic cheese
1 tsp Worcestershire sauce
red pepper to taste
1 cup bread crumbs (optional)

Cook the spinach according to the directions on the package. Drain and reserve liquid.

Melt the butter in a saucepan over low heat. Add flour, stirring until blended and smooth, but not brown. Add onion and cook until soft but not brown.

Add liquid slowly, stirring constantly to avoid lumps. Cook until smooth and thick; continue stirring.

Cut cheese into small pieces.

Add seasonings and cheese. Stir until melted.

Combine with cooked spinach.

This may be served immediately or put into a casserole dish and topped with buttered bread crumbs. The flavor is improved if the latter is done and dish is kept in refrigerator overnight, then reheated. Can be frozen.

Au Gratin Potatoes

To please the grandkids, Grandma Lila Faust added this to her Swedish Christmas, and it's a hit with everyone.

SERVES 12.

   1 2-pound package frozen hash browns
   2 10³/₄-ounce cans condensed cream of mushroom soup
   1 small finely diced onion
   1 green bell pepper, minced
   1 8-ounce container sour cream
   1¹/₂ cups shredded cheddar cheese

Preheat oven to 300 degrees F. Grease a 9 × 13-inch baking pan.

Spread frozen hash browns into the bottom of the prepared pan. Mix together soup, onion, green bell pepper, sour cream, and cheese; pour the mixture over the potatoes.

Bake for 45 minutes.

Green Beans With Roasted Hazelnuts

From the files of Maurine Peterson.

MAKES 8 SERVINGS.

   ¹/₃ cup toasted hazelnuts, chopped
   1¹/₂ pounds green beans (frozen is fine)
   2 tbsp unsalted butter
   ¹/₂ tsp salt
   pepper to taste

Preheat oven to 350 degrees F.

Place the hazelnuts on a baking sheet and bake for about ten minutes, stirring occasionally. When finished, rub with a dish towel to remove the skins.

If using fresh beans, bring a large pot of water to boiling, add beans, and cook for about 8 minutes or until tender-crisp. Drain.

Heat the butter in a small pan until golden brown and fragrant, about 3 minutes.

Place the beans in a serving dish and toss with butter, salt, and pepper. Sprinkle nuts on top and serve.

Swedish Rutabaga

A smorgasbord essential!

MAKES 6 SERVINGS.

> 2 medium rutabaga, pared
> butter
> salt and pepper to taste

Cut pared rutabagas into quarters and then into slices about ¼-inch thick. Cook in boiling salted water until tender—about 15 minutes.

Toss with butter, salt, and pepper, and serve.

Olga's Pineapple Soufflé

From the files of Olga Simon. For those with a sweet tooth. Incredible!

SERVES 10.

> ½ pound sweet butter, softened
> ½ cup sugar
> 4 eggs
> 1 20-ounce can crushed pineapple
> 5–7 slices white bread (crusts removed), diced

Preheat oven to 350 degrees F.

Beat butter and sugar well.

When creamed together, add eggs and beat again.

Add pineapple, including juice. Mix in cubed bread.

Pour into a greased 9 × 11-inch pan and bake at for 1 hour, or until slightly brown.

SAUCES AND CONDIMENTS

Orange Chocolate Fondue

We have yet to run across a family member or friend who wasn't mad about chocolate fondue!

MAKES 6 CUPS.

> 32 ounces good dark chocolate, grated
> 1¼ cups heavy cream
> 1 tbsp orange extract
> 1 tsp white sugar
> ⅓ cup hot water

In a medium saucepan over medium heat, melt together chocolate and heavy cream. Mix in the orange extract, sugar, and hot water. Continue to heat, stirring frequently until the mixture has thickened.

Once heated through, place fondue pot over burner—keeping heat low so the chocolate doesn't scorch. Using fondue forks, dip fruit, shortbread, or your favorite Christmas cookies into the mixture. Also great as a sauce over ice cream.

For a crowd-pleasing variation try replacing the orange extract with one of the following:

> 1 tbsp vanilla extract
> 1 tbsp almond extract
> ½ tbsp peppermint extract

Spicy Sweet Sauce

This sauce is perfect served over apple pie, pancakes, cinnamon rolls or on the Pecan Crusted French Toast.

MAKES 1 CUP.

> $^2/_3$ cup white sugar
> $^1/_3$ cup light corn syrup
> $^1/_4$ cup butter
> 2 tsp ground cinnamon
> $^1/_8$ tsp ground cloves

In a medium saucepan, combine all ingredients. Cook over low heat until the sauce comes to a boil. Cool slightly and serve warm.

Cranberry Apple Sauce

A terrific side.

> 12 ounces cranberries
> 6 ounces unsweetened apple juice concentrate

In a medium saucepan, mix together cranberries and apple juice concentrate. Cook over medium heat until cranberries have burst. Chill and serve.

BREADS AND DESSERT

Crown your feasts with rock hard loaves of fruit cake and enough sweets and cakes to rot the teeth of an entire family. For many, this is the only time of year when one can have sweet rolls for breakfast, lunch, and dinner.

Christmas Graham Cracker Rolls

No Christmas brunch is complete without these tasty morsels! From the Christmas traditions of Aimee Schnabel. (Originally from the kitchen of Vicki Petersen Moras, Aimee's Cajun stepmother.)

MAKES ABOUT FOUR 3–4-INCH ROLLS.

> 1 box graham crackers
> 1 can condensed milk
> 1 cup pecans, chopped
> 1 cup raisins
> 1/2 cup maraschino cherries, chopped
> 1 tbsp cherry juice from cherry jar

Grind the crackers. Set a small amount aside. Mix the remaining ingredients and add to the ground crackers. Shape into a log. Roll the completed log in the reserved crumbs. Wrap in wax paper and store in the refrigerator. (It should be at least the night before so it can chill.)

Slice in rounds to serve.

Great Great Grandma Schwab's Boiled Fruit Cake

This recipe has been passed down in Jessica's family for years. It is her Grandma Rose's grandmother's special cake.

1 cup brown sugar
1 cup water
¹/₂ cup butter and lard mixed (you can use shortening in place of lard)
1 cup dates
¹/₂ tsp each cinnamon, ground cloves, nutmeg, allspice

Place all the ingredients together in a large pan and boil for 3 minutes.

When finished add:

2 cups flour
¹/₂ cup chopped walnuts
¹/₂ tsp baking soda
¹/₂ tsp lemon extract

Stir together and bake for 1 hour at 350 degrees F.

German Gingerbread

This delicious treat can be made into a gingerbread house, gingerbread boys or girls, or just round cookies.

2¹/₂ tbsp Karo syrup
¹/₂ cup butter
¹/₂ cup brown sugar
1 egg yolk
2 cups flour
1 tsp baking soda
3 tsp ground ginger
dash of cinnamon
extra flour for rolling pastry
currants, orange peel, cherries, candies, and icing for decorating

Stand the container of syrup in hot water to soften.

Beat the butter and sugar to a cream, then beat the egg yolk and syrup. Slowly add flour, baking soda, ginger, and cinnamon.

With floury hands, knead into a dough. Wrap in plastic and chill for 1 hour.

Preheat oven to 350 degrees F.

Brush flour on the rolling pin and on the table or counter. Roll the dough to about ⅓-inch thick and cut out into desired shapes.

Place on a cookies sheet and bake for about 12 minutes. Decorate!

Rum Cake

From the files of Lila Faust.

> 1 cup chopped pecans
> 1 package yellow cake mix (make sure *not* to use the cake mix with pudding)
> 1 package vanilla-flavored instant pudding and pie mix
> ½ cup water
> ½ cup vegetable oil
> ½ cup dark rum (80 proof)
> 4 eggs

GLAZE

> ½ cup sugar
> ¼ cup butter
> 3 tbsp water
> ¼ cup rum

Preheat oven to 325 degrees F. Grease and flour a bundt cake pan.

Sprinkle the nuts evenly in the bottom of the cake pan.

In a large bowl, mix together the cake mix, pudding mix, water, oil, rum, and eggs. Pour into the pan.

Bake for 55–60 minutes. Cool in the pan for 15 minutes, then remove the cake to a plate.

Glaze: Place ingredients in a small saucepan over low heat and simmer until butter and sugar have melted. Drizzle over cake.

Peppermint Ice Cream

From the kitchen of Susan McCaffery.

"My family always makes Pink Peppermint Ice Cream in the summer. However, they only use King Leo Peppermint sticks, which you can get at Williams-Sonoma only at Christmas time. It's amazing with chocolate sauce on top and served with brownies."

MAKES 1 GALLON.

> 30 sticks of King Leo Peppermint Candy (16 ounces)
> 15 marshmallows
> milk
> ¹/₂ cup sugar
> 2 (¹/₂-pint) cartons whipping cream
> 1 pint half-and-half

Melt candy and marshmallows together in a pan on low heat with just enough milk to cover. Cover and stir frequently until melted.

When melted, add ¹/₂ cup sugar or to taste, whipping cream, and half-and-half. Place in an ice cream maker and mix until firm.

Christmas Pudding

A delicious English favorite shared by Aunt Nicky. Make at least 3 weeks ahead of time since this recipe is best after sitting.

> ¹/₄ pound flour
> 1 tbsp allspice
> 1 tsp nutmeg
> ¹/₂ pound fresh white breadcrumbs
> 10 ounces finely grated suet or 1 cup sweet butter
> ¹/₂ pound soft brown sugar
> 1 pound sultanas

1 pound raisins

8 ounces large-chopped glace cherries

8 ounces large-chopped dried apricots

1 large grated carrot

4 ounces almonds or walnuts

2 ounces ground almonds

4 large eggs

1 glass of brandy

1 glass of orange liquor

dark beer (Guinness) to mix

Mix together flour, spices, breadcrumbs, suet, sugar, fruit, carrot, and nuts. Combine with beaten eggs and alcohol.

Leave overnight in a cool place.

Divide between two buttered Pyrex bowls and cover securely with wax paper, then seal with aluminum foil.

Steam steadily for at least 6 hours, replenishing water as it boils away. (Place each Pyrex bowl in a saucepan filled halfway with water, bring to a boil and steam gently, checking water level frequently.)

Remove the Pyrex bowls from the pans, leaving to cool. Pudding can be stored for up to 3 months.

Flynns' Fabulous Lemon Cake

No Flynn holiday is complete without Jim and Elaine's lemon cake.

1 18¼-ounce package Lemon Supreme Cake Mix (Duncan Hines)

1 cup apricot nectar

4 eggs, beaten well

³/₄ cup vegetable oil

¹/₂ cup sugar

FIRST GLAZE

2 tbsp powdered sugar

2 tbsp fresh lemon juice

SECOND GLAZE

> 2 tbsp powdered sugar
>
> 1 tbsp fresh lemon juice

Preheat oven to 350 degrees F.

Lightly grease and flour a bundt pan.

Combine all ingredients in the large bowl of an electric mixer. Beat well for about 2 minutes. Pour batter into the prepared pan.

Bake for about 1 hour or until a tester inserted in the middle of the cake comes out clean.

Cool cake in the pan on a rack for about 10 minutes. Invert onto a serving platter. Cool completely. When cool, pierce the top of the cake with a toothpick, so the frosting seeps in just a little.

To frost, mix together ingredients for either glaze, and drizzle over cake.

Rice Pudding with Lingonberries

Another Swedish favorite from Lila Faust. If you can't find fresh lingonberries (which are hard to come by outside of the state of Minnesota), look in the jam or canned fruit section of your grocery store for a jar of lingonberry preserves. They work just as well.

> ¾ cup white rice (not precooked)
>
> 1 tbsp lemon juice
>
> 1 quart whole milk
>
> 2 eggs
>
> ⅓ cup sugar
>
> 1 tsp salt
>
> cinnamon

LINGONBERRY TOPPING

> 1 cup sugar
>
> 1 cup water
>
> 1 package or 1 pound fresh lingonberries

Using a strainer, rinse the rice until the water runs clear. Place in the top of a double-boiler with lemon juice and just enough water to cover the rice. Let it come to a boil and cook for 5 minutes. Drain rice in a strainer.

Using the double-boiler again (make sure there is still enough water in the bottom), add milk and rice to the top pan. Cook slowly until the milk is completely absorbed into the rice (this should take at least 1 hour), stirring occasionally.

Once rice is finished, remove from heat.

In a medium bowl use an electric mixer to beat together eggs, sugar, and salt until it is thick and lemon colored. Slowly fold in the rice until it is well blended.

Pour into a serving dish (a clear glass bowl is perfect), and sprinkle with cinnamon. Chill.

Serve in small bowls with lingonberry topping.

Topping: Combine sugar and water in a medium saucepan. Bring to a boil. Add lingonberries, and return to a boil. Reduce heat and boil gently for 10 minutes, stirring occasionally. Cover and cool completely at room temperature. Refrigerate until serving time.

COOKIES AND CANDY

Christmas is that special time of year when you get to make and eat those cookies that you've been craving for the last 365 days. While everyone has old family favorites, a quick look at some of these recipes will guarantee that it's time to add a new cookie to your holiday traditions.

Chocolate Drops

These delicious Christmas cookies come from Jessica's Grandma Rose and are everyone's favorite.

MAKES 5 DOZEN.

> 1 cup semisweet chocolate chips
> 1 cup butterscotch chips
> 1 cup chow mein noodles
> 1 cup unsalted peanuts

Carefully melt the chocolate chips and butterscotch chips in a large pan over medium heat. Once melted, remove from heat and add chow mein noodles and peanuts. Stir just enough so the peanuts and noodles are covered.

Drop by teaspoonfuls onto waxed paper. Allow to harden. These cookies are best frozen or chilled.

Peanut Blossoms

Sent in by Aimee Schnabel, these are from her mom, Renee Lane.

MAKES 7 DOZEN.

> 1 cup granulated sugar
> 1 cup packed brown sugar
> 1 cup butter or margarine
> 1 cup creamy peanut butter
> 2 eggs
> 1/4 cup milk
> 2 tsp vanilla

3¹/₂ cups sifted all-purpose flour

2 tsp baking soda

1 tsp salt

2 10-ounce packages milk chocolate candies (Kisses)

Preheat oven to 350 degrees F.

Cream sugar, butter or margarine, and peanut butter.

Beat in eggs, milk, and vanilla.

Sift together flour, soda, and salt. Stir into egg mixture.

Shape into balls and roll in additional granulated sugar.

Place the balls on ungreased cookie sheets; bake for 8–9 minutes. Immediately press a Hershey's Chocolate Kiss into each cookie.

Starlight Mint Surprise Cookies

This recipe comes from Kim DeRoche. It is originally from Velda Case, Kim's grandmother-in-law.

MAKES 4¹/₂ DOZEN.

3 cups flour

1 tsp baking soda

¹/₂ tsp salt

1 cup butter

1 cup sugar

¹/₂ cup brown sugar, firmly packed

2 eggs

1 tsp vanilla

Chocolate mint wafers (Fannie Mae are the best—¹/₂-inch diameter)

Preheat oven to 375 degrees F.

Sift together flour, soda, and salt. In separate bowl, cream together butter, sugar, and brown sugar. Then blend in the eggs and vanilla. Add the dry ingredients gradually. Mix well.

To shape the dough for easier handling, shape into rolls about 1¹/₂-inch in diameter. Wrap in wax or parchment paper and chill well. Then cut into slices about ¹/₈-inch thick and place on an ungreased cookie sheet. Top each slice of dough with a chocolate wafer, and then top with another slice of dough.

If desired, add a nut half on top.
Bake for 9–12 minutes.

Mom's Christmas Fudge

Fudge is always a special treat, and this recipe from Jessica's mom is the best!

> 1 12-ounce package milk chocolate chips (2 cups)
> 1 cup semisweet chocolate chips
> 1 14-ounce can sweetened condensed milk
> dash of salt
> 1½ tsp vanilla extract

Line an 8- or 9-inch square pan with wax paper. Make sure the paper is smooth so you don't have any creases in your fudge.

Melt chocolate chips and condensed milk in a pan over low heat until smooth. Remove from heat and stir in vanilla. Spread into the pan and chill until firm.

Variations

Peppermint Fudge: Omit the vanilla and replace with ½ tsp peppermint extract and ¼ cup crushed candy canes.

Nutty Fudge: Stir in ½–1 cup chopped walnuts (or any other nuts).

Orange Fudge: Omit the vanilla and replace with 1½ tsp orange extract.

Frances's Peanut Brittle

Sent by Aimee Schnabel.

> 2 cups sugar
> 1 cup light Karo syrup
> 1 cup water
> 2 cups raw peanuts (one might do)
> 1 tsp soda

1 tsp salt

parafin wax

Place sugar, Karo syrup, and water in a large saucepan until it forms a soft ball. Add peanuts and cook, stirring constantly, until peanuts taste done (long time).

Remove from heat. Add soda, salt, and a piece of parafin the size of your thumbnail. Pour immediately on greased tins.

Cranberry Drops

A favorite recipe from Kim DeRoche's grandmother-in-law, Velda Case.

1/2 cup butter

1 cup sugar

3/4 cup brown sugar

1/4 cup milk

2 tbsp orange juice

1 egg

3 cups flour

1 tsp baking powder

1/2 tsp salt

1/4 tsp baking soda

1 cup chopped nuts

2 1/2 cups coarsely chopped cranberries

Preheat oven to 375 degrees F.

Cream butter and sugars. Add milk, orange juice, and egg. Mix well. Sift dry ingredients together and blend well with sugar mixture. Add nuts and cranberries. Drop by teaspoonfuls on greased cookie sheets. Bake for 10–15 minutes.

Mama Potts's (Miss Mary's) Uncooked Mints

Aimee Schabel's great-grandmother shared this recipe with her whole family.

1 1-pound box powdered sugar, sifted

3 or 4 tbsp milk or cream

1 tbsp butter

7 drops oil of peppermint

5 drops food coloring

Knead all ingredients together with your hands. When mixed and firm, cut into little squares.

Store in a tightly fitted tin for a week to mellow.

Michael's Favorite Peppermint Bark

Next to Grandma Rose's Chocolate Drops, this is Michael Flynn's favorite Christmas recipe.

2 pounds white chocolate

12 candy canes

$^1/_2$ tsp peppermint extract

Cover a jelly roll pan or cookie sheet with waxed paper.

Break up the candy canes into small pieces. The best way to do this is place them all in a ziplock bag and crush with a rolling pin. Be careful not to poke holes in the bag.

Slowly melt the chocolate over low heat until smooth. When chocolate is melted, remove from heat and add candy pieces and peppermint extract.

Spread peppermint chocolate mixture on the pan and chill. Once hard, break bark up into manageable pieces. Serve chilled.

Oatmeal Bars

These terrific bars are one of the few things Jessica's Grandma Rose will make when it isn't Christmas—much to everyone's delight.

4 cups oatmeal

1 cup brown sugar

$^1/_2$ cup shortening

$^1/_2$ cup butter

$^1/_2$ cup white Karo syrup

$^3/_4$ cup chunky peanut butter

1 (12-ounce) package semisweet chocolate chips

Preheat oven to 350 degrees F.

Mix the oatmeal, brown sugar, shortening, butter, and Karo syrup together in a 10×15-inch cake pan. Spread evenly and bake for no longer than 15 minutes.

Melt the peanut butter and chocolate chips together in a saucepan over medium heat. When the bars are done, spread chocolate mixture over them and put in the refrigerator to set.

Mary Beth's English Toffee

An addictive Christmastime favorite from Mary Beth Stanne. Better than a Heath Bar.

> pecans (³/₄ cup, chopped, divided)
> ¹/₄ pound (1 stick) butter
> ¹/₂ cup and 1 tbsp sugar
> 2 tbsp water
> 1 cup semisweet chocolate chips

Lay aluminum foil on a wooden board. Sprinkle half the pecans on foil to cover an area of approximately 8 × 6 inches.

Melt butter over medium-low heat.

When melted, add sugar and water. Turn heat to high and stir *constantly* until mixture turns toffee colored. (Hint: It should start to smoke slightly.)

Pour the mixture over the nuts and spread to cover.

Sprinkle with the chocolate chips.

When the chips melt, spread the chocolate to cover the toffee base.

Finely chop remaining pecans and sprinkle over the top.

Cool at room temperature and store in an airtight container.

Family Favorites

Everyone has favorite recipes that are only eaten at Christmas. Make sure yours don't get lost to the ages and jot them down here to share with generations to come.

RECIPE _____

SERVES _____

_____

_____

_____

_____

_____

_____

_____

_____

_____

_____

_____

❦

RECIPE _____

SERVES _____

_____

_____

_____

_____

_____

_____

_____

_____

_____

_____

_____

RECIPE _____

SERVES _____

_____
_____
_____
_____
_____
_____
_____
_____
_____
_____
_____
_____
_____
_____

✻

RECIPE _____

SERVES _____

_____
_____
_____
_____
_____
_____
_____
_____
_____
_____
_____
_____
_____
_____

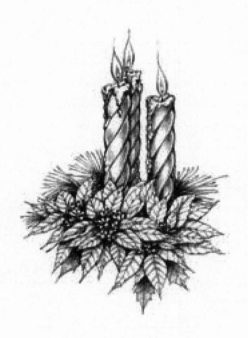

4

Decorating Your Christmas Cottage

Never worry about the size of your Christmas tree.
In the eyes of children, they are all 30 feet tall.

—**Larry Wilde**

One of the more enjoyable aspects of Christmas is that we no longer just decorate a tree. These days, people take Christmas decorating to new extremes, leaving no corner or tree untouched. This chapter will give you tips on decorating not only the inside of your home, but also the tree, the table, and every bush. Use some of the ideas here, along with your own imagination, to turn your home into a Winter or Christmas Wonderland.

Picking a Theme

Everybody has special ornaments and favorite Christmas decorations that come out year after year. But why not make this year different? Instead of the same old, same old, why not pick a special Christmas theme to decorate not only your tree, but your entire house? Here is just a short list of suggestions. Be creative; come up with some of your old ideas. Take a look at your favorite ornaments or decorations and see how you can make this Christmas stand out from all the others.

When picking a theme, keep in mind you can do as little or as much as you want. Some people just coordinate the wrapping paper with the mantel decorations, but keep the same ornaments, stockings, and other decorations year after year. Other people completely change their entire motif each year, matching wrapping paper, ornaments, stockings, mantel decorations, and even the wreath on the outside of the door. If you are someone who likes to go all the way, you can spend as much or as little money as you like. Buy enough ornaments to cover the entire tree or go for the minimal look, and instead of using store-bought ornaments, use ribbons and handmade decorations, or even just colored lights.

White Christmas

A close friend of the Faust family believes in the idea of a White Christmas all year round. Not only is everything in her house white (no color is allowed), but all of her Christmas decorations follow this theme. White Christmas ornaments, stockings, tree skirt, wrapping paper, and even mantel decorations. If a White Christmas isn't up your alley, why not make it a Red, Silver, or even Gold Christmas? Pick your favorite color and run with it.

It's a Multicolored World

If monochromatic doesn't appeal to you, then pick two or three colors and decorate your entire house that way. Almost everyone thinks of red and green at Christmas, but that's the obvious choice. Why not blue and silver, red and gold, gold and burgundy, black and white, purple and silver, or even blue and yellow? You could also decide to use only pastels, primary colors, neons, or metallics.

Pitter Patterns

Just as colors can make a splash in your decorating, choosing a special pattern can be not only fun, but sure to get "oohs" and "ahs" from family and friends. Pick plaids, polka dots, stripes, or even checks. Coordinate your wrapping paper with ribbons wrapped around your tree. One of the prettiest trees we've ever seen was simply decorated with straw ornaments and plaid bows and of course plaid wrapping paper to match.

So Shapely

Everything doesn't have to be about color, you know, so why not go with a shape or motif instead? Growing up in a Swedish household, Jessica was often inundated with hearts. The Christmas tree could easily have stayed up until Valentine's Day, it was so full of love. But hearts aren't the only choice— what about stars, snowflakes, candles, or Santas? There are also gingerbread men, angels, elves, snowmen, and even reindeer.

Remembering Your Heritage

Since America is considered a melting pot, many people choose to use their heritage as a Christmas theme. Whether you are of Russian, South African, German, or Brazilian descent, the traditions and art of these countries can make beautiful and original decorations. It's also a great way to get the entire family to learn more about where you come from. Research the holiday traditions in the country of your choice and find out how that culture not only celebrates Christmas, but also decorates for Christmas. Instead of stockings, you might use wooden shoes, and Santa might be wearing a white cloak instead of a red suit.

My Country, 'Tis of Thee

It's amazing how the tastes and styles of people from the same country can differ so much. Whether you are in the Midwest, Southwest, Northeast, or Amish Country, you'll find that people have a different style of living and decorating based on where they call home. Use these styles as a fun Christmas decorating theme. Pick a region or even a state and honor it with everything you do. You can decorate in Santa Fe colors, buy a large cactus instead of a pine tree, and hang moccasins from the mantel instead of stockings for a fun Southwest theme. Or honor your home state or city. For example, if you are from New York City, you can celebrate by decorating with replicas of the Empire State Building, the Statue of Liberty, and designing your tree so it resembles the Rockefeller Center Christmas tree.

A Biblical Approach

It seems that as time goes on, the true meaning of Christmas often gets lost in the pictures of Santa, cartoons of Frosty the Snowman, or a Rugrats holiday special. Renew the observation of the birthday of Jesus by using a Biblical theme throughout your house. Decorate with a nativity scene, angels, Noah's ark, and stars.

Historical Happenings

A lot of the traditions and even decorations we now use for Christmas come from many different times in not just our country's history, but also world history. Why not use this as a terrific theme for your Christmas? Pick your favorite time period—colonial, Wild West, the Roaring Twenties, Victorian, Art Deco, 1960s tie-dye, or even a futuristic theme—and let your imagination run with it. For example, pick a 1950s or '60s theme and search the Internet for an aluminum tree and use *Leave It to Beaver* ornaments.

Pop Culture

Pop Culture is an especially popular theme if you have kids. Whether you like Bugs Bunny, Mickey Mouse, Rugrats, Snoopy, Barbie, Star Trek, or Elvis, you're bound to find ornaments, tree skirts, stockings, and every other imaginable decoration for your Winter Wonderland.

A Cooking Christmas

Using cooking as a Christmas theme is a great idea for someone who loves to cook. Decorate your tree with gingerbread men, strings of popcorn and candy, cookie cutters, and even toy cooking utensils. Instead of stockings use oven mitts and fill bread pans with candles for your mantel.

A Natural Holiday

Few things are more perfect on a Christmas tree than small birds, bird nests, birdhouses, dried flowers, vines, evergreens, pinecones, nuts, and berries. Since these things actually belong on a tree, they make natural and beautiful ornaments. Decorate the mantel with greens or fresh holly and make your own wrapping paper.

An Entertainer's Dream

Whether you're a book or music lover, or into plays and movies, turning your favorite entertainment into a decorative theme is fun and easy. Use sheet music or photocopied pages of books for wrapping paper and buy ornaments to signify Dickens's *A Christmas Carol*, *The Twelve Days of Christmas*, *It's a Wonderful Life*, or *The Nutcracker*. For the true perfectionist, you can even serve Christmas dinner based on what's eaten in your favorite book, song, or movie.

Winter Sports

Popular with kids and adults alike, winter hats, mittens, scarves, ice skates, sleds, and skis all make perfect Christmas decorations—whether you hang miniatures on the tree or use the real thing as a coffee table.

Other theme ideas to consider include:

Your favorite hobby
Honoring your pet
An ode to your favorite season
Celebrating vacations past
An historical Christmas

Setting the Table

Whether you celebrate Christmas with a formal dinner, a breakfast, or a casual buffet meal, it is usually a time when friends and family gather to eat copious amounts of tasty treats.

If you are the one doing the cooking, don't downplay the time spent in the kitchen by just throwing any old plates and napkins on the table. Now is the time to impress. Pull out your good china and fanciest linens and use them to set a proper and beautiful table.

This may be the only time of year that you get to set a table with both wine and water glasses, bread plates, and soup bowls. So do it! Don't be intimidated by what Great-Aunt Nancy might say. By following these simple tips and diagrams, you'll be on your way to a spectacular table in no time.

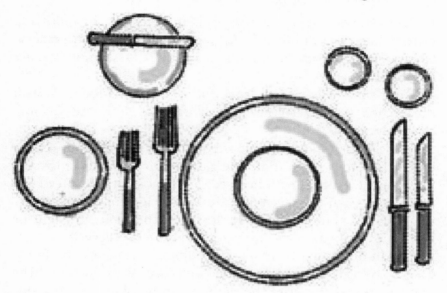

The best way to plan your table setting is to start from the center and work your way out. That means plates. Obviously your dinner plate goes first. If you have a charger, that should go under the dinner plate, although few people actually use chargers these days. If you don't have chargers, but would like to add a special touch to your table setting, check out some of the ideas presented further on in this chapter.

A charger is essentially a decorative platter that sits under the dinner plate and adds pizzazz to the table. It has no function other than to hold a place setting and dress up a table.

The side plate or salad plate should be placed directly to the left of the place setting, and the bread and butter plate should be placed just above the forks.

When placing silverware on the table, it is important to remember one key rule—place them in the order you will use them, from the outside in. Forks should go on the left and spoons and knives on the right. Place spoons and knives together with knife blades pointing toward the plate. Fork prongs should point upward.

From the outside in, forks should be placed in the following order: salad fork, dinner fork, and dessert fork if necessary. Spoons should go on the outside of the knife (assuming you are having soup).

If possible, it is best to leave forks or spoons for dessert in the kitchen. It will keep the clutter down and eliminate washing clean silver.

Wineglasses should be placed at the tip of the main-course knife. If there is more than one glass (wine or water), arrange them in the order they'll be used, outermost first. Coffee cups and saucers can be placed directly to the right of the place setting; however, to keep clutter down on the table, it might be best to leave them in the kitchen until dessert is served.

If you are going to fold your napkins in one of the fancy designs we talk about later, you can place them on top of the main plates. Otherwise, the napkin can be placed on the side plate or to one side of the glasses.

Setting the Buffet

While some families prefer a fancy sit-down meal, others are happiest with a mingling all-day buffet. Depending on your family, or the size of your crowd, a buffet might be the perfect answer. However, just because you are doing a buffet doesn't mean you have to give up an attractive table.

One of the key ingredients to building a beautiful buffet table is elevation. Don't just throw all your platters and bowls on the table, give them some height. Use blocks of wood, upside-down bowls, upside-down flowerpots, boxes, or anything else you can find to put your serving platters of turkey and bowls of mashed potatoes on. Just make sure the block is sturdy enough that your bowl is secure and won't topple once people dip their spoon into it.

The best way to put the table together is to find a tablecloth that is too big for your buffet table (use two tablecloths if necessary). Place your elevation stands under the cloth so they are hidden. Obviously the bowls and platters at the back of the table should be raised and the ones in front can actually be sitting on the table itself.

And don't forget your decorations. Buy some cut flowers, dry some leaves, or tuck bunches of holly in those spaces between bowls to give your table some color. Use garlands, pine boughs, or cranberry strings, and wind them through the bowls and serving platters to add some splashy color and Christmas texture to your buffet.

Dressing the Table

When planning your table, it is important to remember that what goes under the plates is as important as the china itself.

If you're lucky enough to have a beautiful table, you might want to replace the tablecloth with festive place mats. Not only do place mats individualize each person's place, but they are a great way to show off your creativity. Instead of the same old white cloth, you can get place mats made from rush, wood, or even brightly colored or beautifully textured fabric, such as velvet. Consider mixing and matching some of the place mats you already have, or get the kids together to make a special place for everyone.

Other ideas for fun place mats include the following:

- Make Santa hats out of red and white felt. Using a piece of red felt, cut a triangle 26 inches wide at the base and 14 inches tall at the tip. Use white felt to make a round ball, or use a white pom-pom ball for a 3-D effect. Glue the ball to the point of the hat.
- Using the same measurements for the Santa hat, make a Christmas tree place mat out of green felt. If desired, buy different colored felt to make round balls or ornaments to glue on each tree.
- Ask the kids to draw a special Christmas place mat for each guest. Preserve the picture by placing it between a colored backing (construction paper works well) and a piece of clear contact paper. These place mats can also double as place cards.
- Use wrapping paper from Christmases past. Place a piece of wrapping paper between a colored backing (construction paper works well) and a piece of clear contact paper.

These original place mats will make everyone smile when they sit down to dinner.

- Finally put those old Christmas cards to use. Cut them out—pictures and sayings—and place them between a colored backing (construction paper or tagboard work well) and a piece of clear contact paper.

For the more traditional approach, or if you are concerned about the damage hot plates and little fingers can cause, a tablecloth is probably the way to go. But don't feel like you have to use the same white linen your mother and grandmother used. Get creative. What about a red or green cloth to celebrate the season or one with holly embroidered into the cloth? These days it's easy to find inexpensive Christmas tablecloths covered with Santas, holly, or Christmas trees.

If you don't have the money to buy a brand-new tablecloth, go to the nearest fabric store and buy an expensive piece of Christmas cloth. You can either place it over an existing cloth or use it on its own.

When choosing a patterned tablecloth, it's important to keep in mind that patterns can be tricky. If you have patterned china or plan to have an elaborate centerpiece, it might be best to stick with a simple tablecloth or place mats.

Napkins

There is nothing wrong with using paper napkins for Christmas (especially if you have a lot of people or you really liked the Santa design), but for those who really want an elegant dinner, cloth is the way to go. If you decide to use one of the fancy folds below, you should be sure that your napkins are well starched and can hold their shape without wire support.

Bow-Tie Fold

1. Begin with your napkin flat in front of you.
2. Fold the napkin diagonally with the point facing you.
3. Beginning at the tip, slowly roll the napkin into a tube.
4. Taking the ends, tie in a gentle knot.
5. If desired, you can stick a sprig of holly into the knot.

Log Cabin Fold

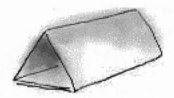

1. Begin with your napkin flat in front of you.
2. Fold the top of the napkin down until it meets the center.
3. Fold the bottom of the napkin halfway up so that it meets the top half.
4. Take the right side of the napkin in your right hand and fold until it meets the center.
5. Do the same with the left side of the napkin.
6. Fold the napkin in half left to right along the crease.
7. Lift the napkin up at the center and allow the two folds to drop down.
8. If desired, place a pine bough or holly leaves in your log cabin.

Wave Fold

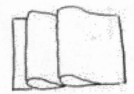

1. Begin with the napkin lying flat in front of you.
2. Lifting the edge closest to you, fold the napkin until it meets the center.
3. Lifting the outer edge again, fold up to the top of the napkin. Crease.
4. Take the left edge of the strip and loosely fold it so the edge reaches the middle of the napkin.
5. Placing your left hand under napkin at the center point, slowly lift and bring the center of the napkin over to the right edge.
6. Fluff the folds to make a wave.

Place Cards

Flower and Spice Place Cards

Makes 8 place card holders.

    Approximately 40 4-inch-long cinnamon sticks
    Floral tape
    Glue gun and glue
    Assortment of small dried flowers (larkspur, statice, lavender, or
        miniature rosebuds work well)
    Small pinecones
    $1/4$-inch-wide velvet ribbon
    $3/4$-inch-wide grosgrain ribbon
    Place cards or $3^1/2$-inch x $3^1/2$-inch white card stock, folded in half

Using floral tape, bind together five cinnamon sticks. Make sure you wrap them in the center of the stick so the tape can be easily covered with a ribbon. Be sure to keep the bottom of the bundle flat so that the place card holder won't roll around when it's placed on the table.

Dip each flower in glue and place along the top of the cinnamon stick bundle. Apply the flowers so that the stems are in the middle and the flower heads are on the outside.

Wrap the velvet ribbon around the bundle and tie a bow. Add a small bow of grosgrain ribbon on top of velvet bow. Glue a few small flowers and a pinecone to the knot portion of your bow.

Insert a place card with the name of the guest into each cinnamon stick bundle.

Felt Place Cards

Makes 8 place card holders.

Glue gun and glue
An assortment of felt pieces in various colors
Scissors
Place cards or 3¹/₂-inch x 3¹/₂-inch white card stock, folded in half

Cut various Christmas shapes out of the felt—Santas, bells, trees, stars. Glue the shapes to the side of each card and write the name of your guests onto the cards.

Alternative: You can also use pretty store-bought gift tags as place cards. Some of the gift tags on the market today are very elegant and lovely.

A Gifted Place Card

Place a small wrapped gift at each place setting. The names on the packages will let your guests know where they should be seated. Gifts could include a small package of homemade cookies, a Christmas ornament (homemade or store-bought), or small bags filled with homemade Christmas candy or nuts.

Santa and Tree Place Cards

The following patterns not only make great place cards, but are also terrific projects to keep children busy while the adults are working in the kitchen. Simply make photocopies (use heavier stock paper if possible) of the pattern. Cut the pattern out on the dotted lines and fold the card on the middle solid line. Then hand the kids crayons or markers and let them decorate to their hearts' content.

Reserved for

Merry Christmas!

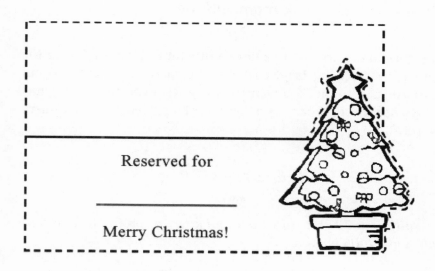

Reserved for

_____

Merry Christmas!

Napkin Rings

Hand-painted Napkin Rings

Plain wooden napkin rings
Acrylic paints
Paint brushes
Glitter

Give each napkin ring its own particular theme. Paint snow-flakes, Christmas lights, small Santa hats, or just a swirl of colors.

Wheat Napkin Ring

Using floral wire, tie together three stems of clean wheat (can be purchased at a craft store) in a fan shape. Using a hot glue gun, attach a small sprig of greenery and pine cones to the center. Place on top of a rolled-up napkin and use a piece of red raffia to attach the wheat to your napkin.

Ornament Ring

Buy special ornaments to match your table décor or fitting for your guests. Using bright ribbon, tie each ornament around your rolled napkin. Your Christmas guests can take the ornaments home with them as a special memento of your wonderful meal.

Beaded Napkin Ring

A beautiful addition to any table and a terrific project to keep both kids and adults busy.

> 24-gauge beading wire (choose gold- or silver-tone to match your decorating motif)
> Variety of jewelry or craft beads in desired shapes, colors, and textures
> Small flat-nose pliers with a cutting edge
> Small round-nose pliers

Using the needle-nose pliers, cut a piece of wire about $6\frac{1}{2}$ inches in length. Using the round-nose pliers, grab the wire about $\frac{1}{2}$ inch from one end and rotate your hand down. Twist around the $\frac{1}{2}$-inch excess wire to create a small secured loop (hangman fashion).

Once your small loop is finished, begin adding beads to the rest of the wire. Create a pattern or just allow the beads to fall where they land. Make sure that when you finish, there is enough wire on the end to secure the ring—about 4 inches of beads should be enough.

Take the open end of wire and thread it through the loop on the opposite end. Twist the wire to secure your ring.

Wreath Napkin Rings

You can also purchase miniature wreaths from your local craft store and use these as napkin rings. Or make your own with little pieces of pine bough from outside and tie together with decorative ribbon for a very festive look.

Centerpieces

An easy and attractive centerpiece can be made by placing a large, decorative bowl in the center of your table and filling it with assorted colored Christmas balls or old-fashioned colored Christmas light bulbs.

For the holiday of giving, why not use a pile of gifts as the centerpiece? You can either use actual gifts that your guests can take home at the end of the meal or wrap empty boxes in paper that reflects your decorating theme. Place the gifts in a decorative container like a sleigh or basket, or simply a base of fresh pine greens.

Place about five bare twigs (collected from your yard) in a vase filled with cranberries (to hold the twigs up). Use small ornaments to decorate the twigs. Winterberry also makes a beautiful and festive flower arrangement. Or collect twigs from the yard and spray-paint them white and tie little red bows on the branches. Lovely!

Yule Log

Take a small birch log and drill four holes in the top. (Before drilling make sure you know which way the log lies best—without rolling around.) The holes should be big enough to hold a taper candle snugly. Once the holes are drilled, decorate the log by using glue or a staple gun to attach holly leaves, evergreen bows, ribbons, or tinsel. This beautiful Yule Log makes a spectacular centerpiece.

Evergreen Centerpiece

A long-lasting centerpiece that can decorate your table for days.

Floral foam and container
1 bunch fresh cedar boughs
Variety of evergreen branches

15–20 ornaments on wires or picks

Ribbon, wire garland, or holiday picks

1–3 candles (optional)

Start by preparing your foam. If you didn't buy your foam and container together, you will need to cut the foam to your container's size. Use a knife and carefully cut the foam so there is at least a 1/2-inch space between the foam and the sides of your container. When shaping your foam, make sure it stands about 1 inch higher than the edges of the container.

Your container should have teeth in the bottom to hold the foam in place. If not, use floral tape to secure it.

To ensure that your centerpiece stays fresh, you will need to make openings for water. In about five to ten places, stick a small knife into the foam and twist slightly to make a small "x"-shaped hole. This will help water get deep inside the foam.

Once your foam is secured into the container, slowly add water. Before building your arrangement, the foam should soak for at least 20 minutes to an hour. The longer you soak the foam, the fresher your arrangement will be.

Now you can begin by inserting your candles. Depending on the size of your foam, you can probably use anywhere from one to three candles in any color. If you're having difficulty, use a knife to make holes big enough to support your candles. Insert candles at least 1 inch apart so the heat from one candle doesn't melt the others.

Taking your cedar boughs, gently remove the last few needles closest to the "stem." This will give you a clean end to insert into the foam. When inserting the boughs into the foam, make sure they arc downward so the ends touch the table and the foam is well hidden. Continue adding cedar and evergreen boughs until you can no longer see the foam.

With the evergreen boughs secured, it is time to add decorations. Try fresh flowers, inexpensive wire garlands, or wired glass ornaments.

Flowers and Plants Ideal for Holiday Centerpieces

Christmas bush

Christmas bells

Holly

Leucodendrum

Strelitzia

Calla lilies

Lisianthus

Pastel statice

Winterberry

Pretty Place Settings

Dinner Wreath

Arrange sprigs of fresh greenery in a circle beneath each place setting. Make sure the wreath is big enough to just peek around the edges of the bottom plate or charger.

All That Glitters

Sprinkle glitter or Christmas confetti under and on your place setting. Just make sure all the confetti has been removed from plates before you start loading them with food.

Tie One On

Tie ribbons in gold, red, blue, or whatever matches your color scheme, to wineglasses and even silverware.

A Touch of Lace

Buy doilies in whatever color matches your table motif. You'll need them in two sizes—small coaster size and the size that is just slightly larger than a bread or salad plate. When setting the table, place a doily between the dinner plate and the bread or salad plate. Use the small doily between the cup and saucer.

Decorating Inside

It takes more than just a Christmas tree to make your home a Christmas paradise. Fortunately, it doesn't have to take much—stockings hung on the mantel or staircase, electric candles in the windows, or sprigs of evergreen on every table.

Decorating and Caring for Your Christmas Tree

Before choosing your live tree, it is important to do a freshness test. Reaching into the heart of the tree, gently grasp a branch between your thumb and forefinger, and slide your hand along the branch toward you. If the tree is fresh, very few needles should come off in your hand. Next, gently shake or bounce the tree on its stump. Again, you shouldn't see very many needles fall to the ground.

Once you've chosen your tree and brought it home, keep it in a sheltered, unheated area such as a porch or garage to protect it from the wind and sun until you are ready to bring it inside and decorate it.

Before bringing your tree into the house, make a fresh, straight cut across the base of the trunk (about a quarter-inch up from the original cut) and place the tree in a tree stand that holds at least a gallon of water. The tree should be placed in water *immediately* after cutting the trunk. If you wait too long, a seal of dried sap will form over the cut stump, preventing the tree from absorbing water. If a seal does form, another fresh cut will need to be made.

A tree will absorb up to a gallon of water when first cut, so one of the most important tips to ensuring a long-lasting tree is water, water, water. In fact, often daily watering isn't enough. Make sure you check the tree at least twice a day. If you allow the tree to go dry for too many days, the trunk will heal over and won't be able to get the water it needs to last through the holiday season.

Once your tree is set up and the tree stand is full of water, it is time to decorate. Start by adding the lights. This way you won't be knocking off and breaking valuable ornaments. Before placing the lights on the tree, be sure to plug them in, check that they are working, and replace any burnt-out or broken light bulbs. Then, starting from the top of the tree, begin stringing. Hopefully you'll end up with the plug at the bottom rear of the tree, near an outlet.

Once the lights are on, you're ready to decorate with ornaments, tinsel, garland, or whatever your preference may be.

Beyond the Tree

Most people who collect miniature Christmas villages place them under the tree or on a table. Why not go one step beyond and make the village your tree? Build a tiered stand using plywood and cover it with a white cloth or sheet. Then build your village on the stand so it is arranged in a pyramid shape mimicking the traditional Christmas tree form.

Display your Christmas cards! You can do this in a number of ways, by standing them up on tables or on the mantel, hanging them on doors or walls, or displaying them in wire cardholders.

Don't feel confined to a pine tree. Use extra ornaments to decorate any plant in your house. If you have larger plants, wind garland around them or hang small, lightweight ornaments from their branches.

Santa's Workshop

While planning your Christmas decorations choose one room in your house that will be devoted to wrapping Christmas presents. Fill the room with all of your wrapping supplies including wrapping paper, fun ribbon, old leftover ornaments, Christmas cards from last year, and anything else that can be used to liven up a plain old present. Make sure you have lots of boxes, decorative bags for large presents and a container that holds scissors, plenty of tape, and gift tags. Placing all of the supplies in one room not only makes wrapping fun, but also a creative project for everyone. It's also just the beginning to a fantastic decorating idea.

Now that you've filled the room, it's time to decorate it. Get the whole family together and decorate the front of the door to the room (the side facing the hallway). Make a sign that says, "Santa's Workshop, No Admittance" or "Santa's Workshop, Knock Before Entering." Use cotton balls to put snow in the corners of the door and red and white striped ribbon for a "candy cane" border. If you're creative enough you could even make a pretend window with elfin eyes peeking out to see who's there.

When the door is shut everyone will know that a Christmas Elf is busy wrapping their gifts and no one is allowed to enter. Not only will wrapping presents be more fun for everyone, but the idea of a secret room will only make Christmas more exciting for little ones.

Decorating Outside

Using a big red bow, hang a pair of old ice skates on the front door in place of a wreath. Use a small, old-fashioned sled to hang either on the door or on the side of the house just next to the door. Decorate the sled with ribbons, greens, or even paint "Merry Christmas" on the seat. Sleds can often be found in Christmas stores or antique stores.

To greet your guests and your family, hang sleigh bells from the doorknob so the holidays ring with every person who enters your home.

A simple and beautiful outdoor decoration can be created by hanging Christmas balls on smaller trees that have lost their leaves. Use a variety of colors or all one color.

Light your walkway or driveway with paper bag luminaries. Fill a lunch-size paper bag about ⅓ full with sand and place a small votive candle on the sand, making sure to secure the candle in place.

Birdseed Ornaments

Don't just use lights to decorate your outside trees; add ornaments as well. Ribbons, bows, and birdseed not only make great decorations, but are also great activities for kids.

Ribbon
Pinecones
Peanut butter
Birdseed

Cut the ribbon in about 6-inch lengths. Tie each ribbon around the top of the pinecone, making sure it is secure and won't fall off. At the top of the ribbon, tie a loop so you can hang it from a tree.

Using a knife or spatula, coat each pinecone with peanut butter, making sure to fill all the nooks and crannies. When finished, roll the pinecones in birdseed, again making sure to fill all the nooks and crannies. Hang outside from trees and bushes.

Christmas Lawn Art

These art projects can be made in any size. Stand them in your lawn or hang them from trees; they'll make a festive accent to any yard.

^{3}/$_8$-inch exterior plywood
Sandpaper (coarse and medium)
Paint and sealer
Pattern
Electric jigsaw or sabor saw
Paint brushes
Power sander (optional)

Enlarge the pattern of your choice (on pages 89–90) to the size you prefer your lawn ornament to be. The best way to enlarge the pattern is by using a grid. Draw a grid of 2-inch squares on brown grocery sacks (several taped together works well) or directly onto the plywood. Use pencil to be able to fix mistakes. Do the same on a copy of the pattern, or photocopy the pattern onto grid paper. Mark the points where the pattern intersects with each square on the grid, then connect the dots.

If you used paper to create the pattern, you will need to transfer it to the plywood. Do so by taping the enlarged pattern to the plywood and punching tiny holes along the pattern's lines—making sure the holes penetrate the wood. Remove the paper and connect the holes to define your lawn art.

Once your pattern has been established, it's time to cut out your design. Using a hand-held electric jigsaw or sabor saw, slowly and carefully cut along your pattern.

Before any real creating can begin, you need to prepare the surface of your project. Using a coarse (50- to 80-grit) sandpaper, round down the rough curved edges to remove any large splinters. Then sand with a medium (80- to 120-grit) paper to get rid of any extra roughness.

Any holes or cracks in your wood can be filled with wood putty. Let dry, then lightly sand the entire surface with medium sandpaper.

Once the edges are smooth, you should seal the wood with a water-repellent preservative. Let dry for about a week before adding a coat of white primer on both sides of your project. When the primer dries, you might want draw in the details of your design with a felt-tip marker before you start painting.

Now that you've finished the work, you can move on to the fun stuff. Painting! Use your imagination to give life to your creation. Add ornaments to the tree, a hat to your snowman, or paint Santa purple. Use quality exterior latex paints. Not only will they add detail, but they are also the best way to protect outdoor wood projects from wind, snow, and rain.

Paint the back of the figure solid black. One coat will probably be enough. Then you can begin on the front. If using white or light-colored paints like pink, you will probably need a second coat, just to make sure the wood is covered. When all finished, use a small brush to outline the entire design (not just the edges) with black paint. This will take some time and attention but is well worth the effort.

When the paint has dried and your art project has a name (and your signature, of course), it's time to anchor your display in the front yard. A wooden stake or metal fence post can be used to help your artwork stand up. Before pushing the stake into the ground, make sure that it is about one-third taller than your artwork. That way you can drive a third of it into the ground.

Once the post is in the ground, attach your figure by screwing small eye-hooks into the back of your figure and attaching it to the post with strong wire.

TREE PATTERN

SNOWMAN PATTERN

GIFT PATTERN

Favorite Decorations

So often people work hard to create the perfect decorations, love them, and then forget what they did the year before. Secure your memories by taking note of them here.

Decoration Name ———— Year ————

Insert Photograph

What I did to create this:

Decoration Name _____ Year _____

Insert Photograph

What I did to create this:

Decoration Name _____ Year _____

Insert Photograph

What I did to create this:

Decoration Name ——————— Year ———

Insert Photograph

What I did to create this:

Decoration Name ——————— Year ———

Insert Photograph

What I did to create this:

5

Christmas Crafts

The merit of originality is not novelty; it is sincerity.
—Thomas Carlyle

*F*or many people, Christmas crafts are as important as Christmas cookies, Christmas carols, and a Christmas tree. Whether you work together as a family to build an annual gingerbread house or make a gift each year for one special person, crafts can be fun for everyone.

In this chapter, we'll give you ideas for the whole family, no matter what your age or ability. And if you go through all of these and find you're looking for more, review Chapter 4, "Decorating Your Christmas Cottage." While not intended to be a chapter of crafts, we found that much of decorating is really crafting.

So grab your scissors and glue gun and laugh and play. And remember, the beauty of crafts is that they don't have to be perfect; they just have to be from you. We recommend playing Christmas music while you work to truly enter into the spirit of Christmas.

Advent Calendars

When Kim DeRoche was a little girl, her mom and aunts made these special advent calendars. A fun project for adults and kids alike.

2 24 × 35-inch pieces of burlap
1 18 × 20-inch piece of green felt
5 sheets of felt in various colors of your choice
Red pen
Gold cording
Sequins, lace, buttons, any decorative doodads
Velcro
Tacky glue
Dowel rod

Begin with one piece of burlap. This will be the base or background of your advent calendar. The second piece of burlap will be used to sew pockets onto the top and bottom of your calendar.

To make the pockets, begin by cutting 24 squares of burlap approximately 2½ inches by 3 inches. Then carefully sew each square onto your base. One row of eight pockets at the top and two rows of eight on the bottom. Once all the pockets have been sewn on, use a red pen to number them.

Once your pockets are finished, use the piece of green felt to make a tree. Using a fabric scissors or pinking shears, cut the tree so that it just fits between the rows of pockets. You might want to consider cutting a tree out of a piece of paper first and using that as your pattern. Sew the tree to your burlap.

Don't decorate your tree too much (since that's the point of the ornaments in the pockets), but if you desire, you can add gold or silver cording to imitate tinsel. Then use self-stick Velcro or sew small squares of Velcro all over the tree—making sure you have one at the top for the star.

Take the dowel rod and fold the top of the burlap over the rod, sewing or gluing it in place. Tie ribbon or cording at each end of the dowel to hang your calendar.

Once your tree and pockets are complete, the fun really begins. Using any color felt you desire—red, blue, white, and even black—cut circles, squares, triangles, or any shape you'd like your ornaments to be in. Sew a piece of Velcro to the back of each ornament and use sequins, lace, beads, and whatever other knickknacks you have to spiff up the ornaments.

Each ornament goes in its own pocket. And then for every day in December up through the twenty-fourth, an ornament is pulled out of the correctly numbered pocket and hung on the tree (leaving the star until last). When all the ornaments have been hung, you'll know that Christmas has arrived.

Cinnamon Ornaments

A delicious-smelling dough and the perfect craft for adults and kids alike.

1¹/₂ cups ground cinnamon

1 cup applesauce

¹/₃ cup white glue (like Elmer's)

1 medium-sized bowl

Flat surface for kneading

Wax paper

Rolling pin

Cookie cutters—various types

Knife

Straw

Nonstick cooling rack

Ribbon

Paints, optional

Mix together cinnamon, applesauce, and glue in a bowl or old plastic container. When well mixed, remove the dough from the bowl and knead until the mixture turns into a firm clay. Let it sit for about 30 minutes.

Cover your table or counter with wax paper. Use cinnamon to dust your rolling pin, hands, and working surface.

Roll out clay to approximately ¹/₈-inch thick. Use cookie cutters or a glass to cut out desired shapes.

If you plan on using your creations as ornaments, use a

straw to cut out a hole near the top. Place the shapes on a non-stick cooling rack or wax paper. Keep an eye on them and turn occasionally so that they dry evenly and flat. Dry for approximately 5 days.

Once dry, decorate with paint or markers.

Painted Holiday Tiles

Old or new ceramic tiles can be used for a number of things—coasters, trivets, or ornaments. They make great decorations around the house and even better gifts for family and friends.

> Light-colored ceramic tiles—white or off-white is best (available in crafts stores). If the tile is too dark, the paint won't show up.
> Delta CeramDecor Air-Dry
> PermEnamel
> PermEnamel Surface Cleaner and Conditioner
> PermEnamel Clear Gloss Glaze
> $1/4$-inch-wide satin ribbon
> Small sponge
> Paintbrushes
> Felt squares
> Glue gun

Prepare each tile following the instructions on the Surface Cleaner.

Once the tiles have been prepared, you can begin painting. Use the sponge to give a whole new texture. If desired, use a pencil to lightly draw an outline of the image you want to paint (tree, candy canes, snowflakes, Santa, etc.). Then paint the outline of the figure and allow to dry.

Once dry, fill in with whatever colors you desire. Let dry.

Glaze lightly. Let dry.

To use as an ornament, use a strong tacky glue to attach the ribbon to the back of the tile in a loop. Then glue the felt to the back of the tile to cover ribbon.

For coasters or trivets, just glue felt to the back or bottom of the tile.

The Sock Snowman

*Everyone loves a cheery snowman or snowwoman, and these little
guys made from baby socks are adorable and decorative.*

White tube sock (preferably a child's)
Infant's colored ribbed sock
Fiberfill and rice stuffing
2 pipe cleaners, any color but should match
Orange fabric scraps or felt
Felt and fabric scraps for mittens and scarf
Pink marker
¹/₄-inch stencil brush
Black marker
⁵/₈-inch buttons
Glue gun
Pencil

Begin by turning the sock inside out so the terrycloth is on the
outside. Fill with rice until the sock is approximately ³/₄ full.
Tie tightly at the top of the rice with a string (the string is
where the neck will be). Stuff the remaining area with fiberfill
to make the head. Tie off with a string again and trim off the
ends.

Starting at the left (front) side of the neck, wrap the pipe
cleaner to the right, around the front and back of the snowman, to finish with the end sticking straight out, to the left of
the snowman's head. The pipe cleaner should stick straight out
to form the left arm, anchored around the neck. Do the same
with the other pipe cleaner, starting at the right (front) side this
time, and wrapping the pipe cleaner to the left and around the
back to form the right arm.

Cut the orange fabric into a carrot, triangle, or whatever
shape you would like the nose to be in. Using the felt or fabric
scrap of your choice, cut out little mittens. Glue the mittens
and nose on the snowman.

Take the colored sock and cut off the foot part—leaving the
ribbed ankle band for the hat. Glue the cut end closed.

Use the pink marker to paint the cheeks. Draw black-dot

eyes and a mouth with the black marker. With thumbs inward, paint straight white running stitches close to the edges of the mittens.

Glue on the hat. Cut out bottoms from the felt and glue them down the center of the body.

Cut a small piece of fabric—1 × 13 inches—for a scarf and tie it around the neck.

Let the glue dry.

Voilà!

Glass Christmas Tree

These baby food Christmas trees make great gifts. They also work as decorations for a child's room or for someone in the hospital.

33 baby food jars with lids, all the same size
Glue gun
Heavy strength glue
1 strand of small Christmas lights—about 35 lights
Tinsel
Ribbon

Begin by drilling a hole in the top of each jar lid—the hole should be just big enough for a Christmas light socket to fit through. Drill the hole by placing the lid upside down on a block of wood. NOTE: Be careful when drilling the holes. Wear gloves and safety goggles since you are drilling into metal.

Before replacing the lids on the jars, stuff each jar with tinsel. Don't overstuff, since you want the light to shine through, but stuff enough so that you can't see the bare light bulb. About fifteen to twenty pieces work well.

Set the jars on a table with the lid sides up. Start with the bottom of the tree—seven jars. It might be helpful to push the jars up against a flat surface so you can ensure that they are all even with each other. Run a line of glue up the side of each jar and glue them together.

Do the same with 6 jars, 5, 4, 3, 2. Let them all dry overnight.

Once dry, lay the row of seven jars on its side, with the lids facing you and the bottoms backed up against a wall or board. Use your glue to adhere the row of 6 jars to the top. Do the same with the rest of your rows so that they form a pyramid. Let dry overnight.

```
      O
     OO
    OOO
   OOOO
  OOOOO
 OOOOOO
OOOOOOO
```

When finished with your tree pyramid, you can build the trunk by gluing together three jars in one row and two jars in the other. Let dry overnight.

When the tree and trunk have both dried, you can attach the trunk to the tree in the same way you attached the tree rows together, with the two jars on top of the three jars.

```
      O
     OO
    OOO
   OOOO
  OOOOO
 OOOOOO
OOOOOOO
    OO
   OOO
```

If desired, you can glue Christmas ribbon around the perimeter of the tree or just around the base.

When adding the lights to your tree, start at the top and insert a light into the hole of each lid. If desired, you can add a second string of lights or use a longer string and add multiple bulbs to each jar.

When finished, plug in and enjoy!

Christmas Potpourri Pot

1 half-gallon mason jar

1 string miniature Christmas lights

Christmas potpourri (from your local store or craft shop)

Decorative Christmas fabric (use velvet, plaid, or some other festive
fabric)

Decorative holiday ribbon

Fill your mason jar with Christmas lights and potpourri so that lights and potpourri are well mixed together.

Cut out a circle of fabric with which to cover the top of your mason jar. Leave at least 2 inches around so that the fabric hangs down over the rim, covering the rim completely.

Place the fabric over the jar and mark the fabric with a small dot, where you will cut a small hole in the fabric so that you can poke the light string through, enabling you to plug the lights into the wall. (Make sure the cut will be toward the back of the fabric, where the fabric just meets the edge of the jar.)

Cut the hole in the fabric and thread the lights through.

Place the fabric back on the jar, with the lights threaded through. Take your decorative ribbon and tie it around the edge of the jar, securing the fabric on top of the jar and making a pretty Christmasy lid.

Plug in your lights and admire your Christmas potpourri pot!

Candy Cane Candles

An easy project for adults and kids. Also makes a great gift!

1 pillar candle—about the height of a candy cane
Candy canes—you will need them to be about the height of the candle
    and as many as it takes to go around the candle. (If desired, cinnamon
    sticks can be used in place of candy canes.)
Glue
Ribbon

Carefully glue each candy cane vertically around the candle. Allow to dry.

Tie a ribbon around the candle and finish with a bow. Enjoy!

Christmas Present Garland

This beautiful decoration and gift was first made by Carol Kortus and now graces the homes of many of our friends.

6 feet of fake green Christmas garland—better if it's thick and "leafy"
8 clear plastic salad bar or deli containers of all different shapes and
    sizes—clean and dry
White curly ribbon
50-foot strand of small white Christmas lights
Cellophane wrapping paper in various colors
Tape
10-gauge florist wire

Punch two holes in the bottom of each deli container, about 1 inch apart. Take 6 inches of florist wire and slip in one hole and out the other, so the ends are on the outside of the container. Secure with a small piece of tape.

Wrap each deli container with the cellophane as you would wrap a present, using at least three different colors—red, green, yellow, purple, etc. Be careful that the florist wire doesn't come loose or rip the cellophane. Make sure the ends are on the outside of the cellophane.

Tie ribbon around each "present" and curl the top.

Wrap the garland with the Christmas lights.

Attach each present to the garland using the florist wire. You can add as many or as few packages as you wish.

Plug in and watch the presents light up.

Personalized Snow Globes

Everyone loves a snow globe! So why not make one that's extra-special to you, or to the person who is lucky enough to receive this special gift.

A variety of jars—baby food, mustard, olive, etc.

Plastic or ceramic figures or ornaments (look in hobby shops or model-train shops)

Plastic evergreen tips

Oil-based enamel paint in holiday colors

Coarse sandpaper

Epoxy (clear-drying)

Distilled water

Glitter

Glycerin (available at drugstores)

Begin the day before by painting the lids of the jars in holiday colors. Be creative—paint green for grass, red and white stripes, or blue with white polka dots.

When the paint dries, use coarse sandpaper to sand the inside of the lid until the surface is rough. This will ensure the epoxy has a surface to attach to. Using the epoxy, adhere the figurine or figurines to the inside of the lid. This is your chance to get really creative. Create carolers, a snowman, or a forest of animals. Allow the epoxy to dry for a few hours.

Fill the jar almost to the top with distilled water; add a pinch of glitter and a dash of glycerin. The glycerin will keep the glitter from falling too quickly. Be careful not to add too much glitter or it will stick to the bottom of the jar. Screw the lid on tightly, turn the jar over—and let it snow.

Pomanders

These wonderful-smelling decorations have been used since Medieval times. They make not only great ornaments, but fantastic gifts as well.

Oranges, lemons, or limes

Whole cloves

Medium-size nail

Powdered cinnamon, nutmeg, or allspice

Ribbon

A pomander is simply an orange or other piece of fruit studded with cloves. This easy craft will fill closets, cars, or entire rooms with a fresh, clean scent.

Begin your pomander by poking holes into your orange with a nail. Make sure the holes are smaller than your cloves, otherwise you won't be able to get the cloves to stay put. Space your holes as evenly and as close together as possible. You can use the cloves to make a design or just cover your entire orange.

Once your holes are made, start adding cloves. If you'd like, you can add additional fragrance by placing cinnamon, or other spices, in a bag and shaking the pomander inside. Shake gently so you don't dislodge your cloves.

Tie a ribbon around the sides of your pomander with a big bow on top. Hang in a closet, place in a drawer, or hang several around your house for a fresh scent.

Polka-Dot Garland

A pretty addition to any polka-dot theme! Also a great craft for kids and adults and a nice touch to any tree.

> Color-coding round labels (found at any business supply store). *To color labels yourself, buy the white round labels and use felt-tip markers in the colors of your choice.
> Heavy thread (button thread works best).

Begin at one end of your thread and stick your labels back-to-back on the thread. Spacing the dots about 2 inches apart, work from one end to the other.

Use your imagination! Garland can also be made from foil stars, fun stickers, or labels you color yourself.

Christmas Sachet

A simple sewing project for those who can hardly thread a needle.

> Green felt, large enough for two tree patterns
> Needle and green thread
> Stick pins
> Lavender, cedar, or another great sachet scent (fiberfill works for those who don't want a sachet)
> An assortment of buttons and beads
> Ribbon or yarn

Make a photocopy of the tree pattern on page 89 and cut out. If desired, you can use the enlarging option on your copier to make trees of different sizes.

Using the pattern, cut out two identical trees from your felt. You might want to cut both pieces at the same time to guarantee that they will be the same size.

Sew an assortment of buttons and beads onto both trees. Try not to sew any too close to the edge, since that is where you'll have to sew the two trees together. Because the inside will not be visible, you don't have to tie off any threads or worry if it looks messy. No one is going to see it!

If desired, use a piece of ribbon or yarn and sew it to the top of the tree. This will be your hanger.

Once your trees are well decorated, it is time to sew them together. With the button sides facing each other, place the trees together. Use a few pins to secure them, and then stitch around the outside, except for the bottom of the trunk.

When your stitches are secure, turn your tree inside out, through the hole you left opened. You'll want to be sure the hole is big enough to accommodate any of the larger beads or buttons.

Fill your tree with herbs, cedar, or stuffing. Don't overfill; the tree should have just enough stuffing to make it plump.

Once you are pleased with how your tree is stuffed, sew the last part of the trunk closed.

If desired, make your own patterns. You could do a snowman, Santa, or even a star.

Christmas Candleholder

Using old jars, these cute projects are great for all ages.

> Baby food jar (emptied and rinsed out)
> Paint
> Ribbon
> Tea light candle
> Paintbrush
> Glitter pens

Using a clean, dry jar, begin by tying a ribbon around the top, but down from the edge so the flame can't reach it.

Using paints and glitter, decorate the jar in any way you wish. Paint on snowflakes, snowmen, starts, hearts, or trees. Use your imagination!

Place the candle inside and use your holder as a gift or table decoration.

Homemade Cookie Tins

Great for giving cookies or other treats as gifts. Can also be used as pencil holders, for loose change, or as an outside luminary.

> Clean, dry tin cans of all shapes and sizes
> Acrylic paints
> Paint brushes

Use your imagination to paint whatever you want on the cans. Paint on a snowman, Santa Claus, a Christmas tree, or a starry night with Santa's sleigh riding through.

If you wish to use the cans as luminaries, use a drill (and wear goggles) to outline the shape of the painting with spaced dots. When a candle is placed inside, the light will shine through the holes.

Fill with tissue paper and cookies or candy canes for a great gift.

Merry Christmas Doormat

A wonderful way to greet your guests at the door.

Sisal door mat
Ribbon
Bells
Scissors
Large-eye plastic needle

Since the weave of a sisal mat lends itself to cross-stitch, decide on the word (WELCOME, JOY, NOEL, etc.) or pattern you would like to stitch and make sure they will fit. If desired, start by laying out the design on graph paper, with each square representing a square on the mat. Start in the middle so you can ensure your pattern is centered.

Thread a large-eye plastic needle with a piece of ribbon and start cross-stitching the design by coming up from the back through a hole, going down through the diagonal hole, coming up through the hole directly below it, crossing over the last stitch, and going down in the diagonal hole above the first hole, making an X. Continue with your pattern until you see your word take shape.

To decorate the edges of your mat, use an overstitch. To do this, you need to start underneath the mat, and bring the needle up through one of the holes near the edge. Pull the strip through and around the edge, come up from the bottom of the mat, and skip a hole, coming up in the second hole from where you started.

When finished, you can attach small bells or greenery onto the corner of your mat for an added festive touch.

Christmas Serving Tray

The perfect way to start your Christmas breakfast, or a fabulous gift for everyone.

Old greeting cards, photos, postcards, or a child's artwork
Picture frame
Glass or Plexiglas
Cardboard
Thin sheet of plywood
Screws
Screw-in cabinet pulls
Door pulls
Caulk
Caulking gun
Damp cloth

Choose a frame for your tray. The frame you choose should be wide enough to grip and deep enough to keep items from slipping. If your frame doesn't come with glass, have a piece cut to fit inside the tray.

Cut a piece of cardboard to the same size as your glass. Using the cardboard as your backdrop (cover with plain paper, a picture mat, wrapping paper, or something else if desired), lightly glue your items in place. Insert on top of the glass.

Fit a thin piece of plywood over your frame. The plywood must be a little bigger than the back opening so it can be screwed to the back of the frame. Screw the plywood to the back of the frame at the corners and the middle.

Using your door pulls or knobs as feet, screw those onto the four corners of your plywood.

Attach a handle to each end of the tray. Choose handles with holes on the outside, like screen-door pulls, so you can screw them directly in.

Protect your framed art from leaks by applying caulk to the inside edges of the glass. Smooth the caulk into the crack with a damp cloth.

Colorful Fireplace Pinecones

When tossed into a roaring fire in your fireplace, these pinecones will add color to your flames.

The following chemicals can be purchased at a pharmacy—1 pound of each:

Barium nitrate
Copper sulfate
Strontium nitrate
Calcium chloride
Copper chloride
Lithium chloride
Potassium permanganate
A collection of dried pinecones
Rubber gloves
Old newspaper
Disposable pan (the chemicals stain)

Choose the chemical according to the color you would like to make your flames, as follows:

Blue flame = barium nitrate
Bluish flame = copper sulfate
Red flame = stronium nitrate
Orange flame = calcium chloride
Green flame = copper chloride
Purple flame = lithium chloride
Purple flame = potassium permanganate

In the disposable pan, mix 1 pound of the chemical in a gallon of water.

Place your pinecones in a cloth sack and immerse them in the solution for 30 minutes.

Slowly lift the sack out of the water, letting it drip back into the pan as much as possible.

When done dripping, spread cones on thick pad of newspaper until they're dry.

Glass Ball Ornaments

Clear glass ornament balls from your local craft store (any size)

Glass paints (such as Delta Ceramcoat)

Rubbing alcohol

Newspaper

Paper towels

Decorative ribbon or thread for hanging

Remove the ornamental tops from your glass balls. Set aside.

Pour in a small amount (a teaspoonful) of rubbing alcohol into your glass ball and swirl around, making sure the inside of the ball gets covered with the alcohol. Drain into the next ball and continue until all balls are covered. Discard any leftover rubbing alcohol.

Turn ball upside down in plastic tray (use the tray the balls came in) and drain overnight. (This cleans and coats the inside of the ball, allowing the paint to adhere to the surface.)

Before you proceed, make sure the balls are completely dry from the rubbing alcohol.

Pour small amounts of paint inside the glass balls and swirl around, creating a swirl effect and pattern. Gently rotate the ball from side to side, slowly, ensuring that the entire inside gets coated with paint. Alternate colors, depending on your Christmas theme or personal taste. Favorite color combinations are red and gold, blue and silver, red and green, gold and light gold, or pastel combinations. Or get creative and mix your colors together before tipping them into the ball.

When the insides are covered with paint, place topside down so that excess paint can drain out on paper towels or newspaper. Please note that quite a bit of paint might drip out, so be prepared!

Leave the balls to dry for at least one week. Then wipe away excess paint from outside of the balls (from dripping paint) with a paper towel and replace decorative top. Add ribbon to hang the balls from the tree or presents. *Voilà!*

Christmas for Pets

Of course, we won't forget our special furry friends at Christmas. Here are some ideas to make Christmas special for the four-legged family members.

Catnip Kitty Surprise

Catnip
Holiday-theme fabric
Needle and thread
Scissors
Cardboard
Pencil for drawing

Buy a container of catnip from your local pet store and set aside. At your fabric store, find a holiday themed fabric, such as one with candy canes, Christmas trees, or just a green and red design. You most likely won't need more than a ¹/₂ yard of fabric (and this will probably last a few years), but it all depends on how many treats you plan to make.

Draw desired shapes on your cardboard in pencil. These will become the patterns for your Catnip Kitty Surprises. We have found that candy canes, Christmas trees, or just little rectangles, circles, or squares work best. Cut out the shapes you have drawn on the cardboard. We always make them fairly small: Remember, they are for cats to play with! A 1" or 2" inch cutout is plenty big enough.

Set aside your patterns. Fold the fabric in half, design side out. Place the cardboard pattern on top and cut out your shapes so that you have two pieces of fabric per shape (front and back). Place the fabric shapes together, design side in, and sew together leaving one end open for stuffing. Turn the fabric right side out, using a pencil or knitting needle to get the corners just right. Stuff with your catnip and sew the remaining side shut. Your cats will have a very happy Christmas!

Holiday Tug Toy

Most dogs love to play tug. Make your own tug toy at home for an inexpensive but special gift for your canine friend.

Thick nylon rope is all you'll need. Cut the rope into three equal parts. A good length for each piece is 2 feet, so you'll need at least 6 feet of rope. Never use string, and always use a rope thick enough that your dog won't shred it and swallow as it could cause some intestinal damage. Try to buy rope in red and green, or some other nice holiday combination, such as gold and red, or silver and blue. (Buy 4 feet of red and 2 feet of green, or some other like combination.) Braid 3 pieces of the rope together and knot at each end. Now, pull!

Favorite Crafts

Record pictures and directions for some of your favorite Christmas crafts.

Decoration Name _____ Year _____

Insert Photograph

What I did to create this craft:

Decoration Name —————————————— Year ————

Insert Photograph

What I did to create this craft:

Decoration Name _____ Year _____

Insert Photograph

What I did to create this craft:

Decoration Name _____ Year _____

Insert Photograph

What I did to create this craft:

Decoration Name —————— ———— Year

Insert Photograph

What I did to create this craft:

6

Christmas Traditions and Family Fun

It comes every year and will go on forever.
And along with Christmas belong the keepsakes and the customs.
Those humble, everyday things a mother clings to, and ponders,
like Mary in the secret spaces of her heart.

—Marjorie Holmes

While Christmas is celebrated throughout the world, traditions vary greatly from household to household. Whether you already have your own special traditions that you'd like to preserve for years to come, or are looking to add new traditions for your family holiday, this chapter will provide you with insight into other people's traditions as well as give you ideas for starting new family traditions at home.

Christmas Eve Nativity

Take time out from your shopping, gift opening, and celebrating to recognize the true meaning of Christmas. On Christmas Eve, no matter what time you finally arrive home from a Christmas party, Grandma's, or church, gather around your Christmas tree and, as a family, put up your nativity scene.

Choose one person to read the story of Jesus' birth (if you don't want to read directly from the Bible, there are a number of great children's books on the subject). As each character or person is introduced (from Joseph and Mary to the Three Wisemen) add the people to your scene. At the end of the story your scene will be complete and time can be taken to discuss the true meaning of Christmas.

A Present for Jesus

Giving a gift to Jesus is a terrific tradition, and a great way to introduce Christmas to children. At the beginning of December wrap an empty box in your favorite Christmas wrap and slit a hole in the top. Whenever you do anything nice for someone else, write it down on a piece of paper and put it in the box. By Christmas day, the box should be full of things Jesus would like for His birthday. If you don't usually celebrate the religious aspects of Christmas, you can use the same idea, but make it a gift for Santa. It's a wonderful way to teach children the value of giving.

Jesse Tree

A Jesse Tree is a symbol of Jesus' family tree and is usually decorated with ornaments associated with Old Testament events, from creation to the birth of Jesus. In some churches, a Jesse tree is used to collect clothing for the poor. The tree is decorated with hats, scarves, gloves, mittens, socks—any small item of warm clothing.

If desired, a Jesse tree can be made from wooden dowels, or use a small pine tree. Decorations can be made out of cardboard and commonly include:

The Sun   A symbol of Christ's ability to dispel darkness and bring eternal life and light.

The Tablets of the Law   A symbol of the tablets given to Moses on Mount Sinai.

The Key of David   An emblem of authority and power.

Bethlehem   The birthplace of Christ.

The Root of Jesse   Another figure of Christ.

The Star of David   The six-pointed star is the emblem of the Royal House of David.

Jacob's Ladder   A symbol of Jacob's vision of a ladder reaching from heaven to earth, with angels descending and ascending.

Jonah in the Whale   As Jonah remained in the whale three days, so Christ remained three days in the earth after His death.

The Temple   The Temple was God's dwelling place among the Jews of the Old Testament.

The Crown and Sceptre   A symbol of Christ's universal kingship.

The Sword of Judith   Judith used a sword to kill the leader of the Assyrian army and save the Israelite nation.

The Burning Bush   God appeared to Moses in the form of a burning bush, a symbol of the Virgin Birth of Christ.

Noah's Ark   Noah preserved man and animal alike within the Ark.

The Ark of the Covenant   The Ark contained the most precious Gift of the New Law.

The Altar of Holocaust   Sacrifice was offered daily on the Jewish altar of holocaust.

The Apple   A representation of a great Redeemer.

The Paschal Lamb   The "Lamb who takes away the sins of the world."

The Pillar of Fire   God appeared in a pillar of fire to lead His people through the desert.

Manna   A symbol of Christ.

Worship With Others

Experience a new worship tradition during the holidays. Attend a Christmas cantata, a children's Christmas pageant, a choir concert, a Living Christmas Tree presentation, an outdoor Living Nativity scene, a tree-lighting ceremony, or a bell-ringing service. Or try a new church. See how people of other faiths celebrate Christmas.

The Christmas Story

Gather together friends and family and take a moment to read aloud the Christmas Story from either the Bible or one of the many books on the subject.

A Birthday Bash

Bake a birthday cake for Jesus. Light the candles on Christmas day and sing ''Happy Birthday.''

O Tannenbaum

Rather than throwing up the tree and leaving the decorating to Mom or Dad, set aside a specific time each year to decorate the Christmas tree as a family. Make hot cocoa and Christmas cookies, and string popcorn and cranberries for an old-fashioned look. Use this time as a terrific way to make special Christmas memories. Turn off the phone and TV and play only Christmas music.

Ornamental Memories

Find a glass blower or other craftsman and ask her to make a special ornament for each member of the family, from the smallest child to the wisest elder. Have each person's name either painted or molded into the ornament. Then each Christmas, when the family is gathered together, start your Christmas celebration by turning out all but your Christmas tree lights, gathering around the tree and having each person (oldest to youngest) hang his or her special ornament. If desired, you can have ornaments made for those cherished loved ones who have passed on and have them hung by others. Also make sure that each time a new member is brought into the family—whether through marriage or birth—an ornament is presented to them.

Another ornament tradition is to give each family member a new ornament every Christmas. When taking down the tree at the end of the year, make sure each person gets a box for their own special ornaments. Then, when it's time for children to leave home and start their own Christmas traditions, they already have a set of special ornaments filled with holiday memories.

Santa's Special Gift

A great tradition, and a great way to entertain excited children, is to leave one gift unwrapped. A favorite doll for Sadie or a truck for Roscoe left under the tree is always thrilling. That way, when the children arrive at Grandma's, they don't have to wait so long to open presents.

Handel's *Messiah*

Participate in an annual performance of Handel's *Messiah* by joining a choir or attend an event at a local church or theater. If you can't find a production close to home, purchase a CD and spend a quiet evening enjoying the music at home.

Helping Others

Sponsor a needy child, elderly person, or family for Christmas. You can contact your local church or Salvation Army to get the name of someone who could use gifts of toys or food. Even better, invite an elderly person or needy family to share in your Christmas dinner. You can also invite college students or servicemen.

Christmas Artwork

Create your own Christmas cards by using an original piece of artwork created by you, your children, or your grandchildren. If desired, carry the theme through everything you do and have place mats, napkins, or gift wrap made from the drawing.

Buy some commercial clay, such as Sculpey or Fima, and create your own clay ornaments that you can bake in the oven—try snowmen, reindeer, Santa, Christmas trees, elves, angels, or even the puppy from the *Grinch*! Personalize them for each family member and hang them proudly on your tree.

Special Gifts

A great and simple Christmas tradition is to give everyone the same gift. Some people give everyone, adults and children, a gift of pajamas, matching red sweatshirts, Christmas socks, Christmas underwear, or even special shoelaces. Using a fabric marker mark the date somewhere on your gift. What terrific fun you'll have when everyone is sitting around in their new pajamas enjoying a cup of hot cocoa.

Phantom Shopper

Unlike Santa, the Phantom Shopper buys only silly presents. If you like, draw names and everyone becomes a Phantom Shopper. Give fish whistles, flying pigs, or a windup toy.

Make a Gift

So often you hear people complain that the spirit of Christmas is lost in the expensive toys, Christmas wrap, and speed at which you rip through presents. Bring back a little of that spirit with this terrific tradition. At Thanksgiving, or even the previous Christmas, have everyone—old and young alike—place their names in a hat. Draw names and keep them a secret. The only requirement is that the gift you give must be homemade. Have children draw pictures and make them into magnets or frame them for the wall. Adults can make cookies, crafts, or whatever their hearts and abilities desire.

A Caroling Concert

When the shopping is done and the presents are wrapped, take a little time to spread the joy of Christmas to those around you. Invite friends and family over for a caroling party. Collect sheets of Christmas carols (either use those in Chapter 2 or check out some of the resources in the back of the book), make a thermos of hot chocolate or mulled cider, and hit the streets. You'll be amazed not only by the fun you'll have, but by the joy you'll so easily bring to others. If you like, take the giving to people who really need it and carol in a nursing home, assisted living home, or hospital.

Christmas Cards and Letters

The tradition of sending out Christmas cards is almost 200 years old and one that has grown from cards to letters to e-mail cards. Instead of just sending out a card with everyone's name stamped inside, why not use this special time of year to go a step further? Get everyone in the family involved by working together on a detailed Christmas letter. Let each child tell others what their favorite moment of the year was and include everyone's signature. The time you spend together doing the cards will be time you cherish forever.

Love Letters

In the spirit of giving, give the gift of yourself. Sit down to write all those special people in your life—husband, wife, parents, children, and friends—a letter expressing your love for them and your gratitude for their love. When all the gift wrap has been cleared away and memories of toys are long forgotten, your love letter will sit in their hearts forever.

Celebrate Other Traditions

Make Christmas a learning experience for your family. Each year choose a new country's traditions to learn about. Decorate a smaller version of your Christmas tree with ornaments from that country, share in ethnic food, and most important, read a book that tells of this different country's traditions.

Volunteer

Take a moment out of your own Christmas activities to help others with theirs. It is amazing how much children can learn from volunteering in a soup kitchen, caroling at a senior center, or wrapping presents for disadvantaged children.

Photographic Memories

Give everyone, adults and children alike, their own Christmas camera. For older children you might want to actually buy them an inexpensive camera, while disposable cameras work well for younger children. Allow them to take pictures of whatever will remind them most of this year's Christmas—a favorite toy, the tree, the family together . . . When the holiday is over, develop the pictures and ask each child to put together their own Christmas memory book, a book that they'll cherish for years to come. Or take a video of your family each Christmas and watch previous Christmas videos and laugh yourself silly!

The Stocking Exchange

Whether you look in your stockings Christmas Eve or Christmas morning, stick to your guns each year and make the stocking its own special event. Each person should have their own individualized stocking—either homemade or store-bought—and stockings can be filled ahead of time to increase anticipation and excitement. Hang them from the mantel and agonize the kids!

Sometime after Thanksgiving you can also get together to make new stockings and have each family member create someone else's stocking. Get plain red and white stockings from the craft store and decorate with card cutouts, glitter, fabric paints, and beads. Write the family member's name in fabric paint or glitter. You can even glue on photos from over the years to capture wonderful memories of Christmases past. Or use old-fashioned stockings or socks. Stocking stuffers are many times the favored gift items, especially for those little ones who love getting lots of things all at once. Don't forget to add some healthy snacks in the stocking, too, like an apple or some nuts.

Santa's Visit

Ask Dad or Grandpa to dress up in a Santa suit each year. His arrival, with a bag of unwrapped gifts, will be thrilling for old and young alike. You'll be amazed at the excitement of the young children and the twinkle in the eyes of the older children when they start to realize who this Santa really is. The anticipation of Santa's arrival will keep everyone on their toes and the gift will keep them busy until it is time to open the rest of the presents.

Table Dressing

For those you enjoy more formal events, make Christmas extraspecial by making the family dress for dinner. Wear special Christmas outfits and take some time before dinner to make yourself look special and feel loved. Shopping for your special Christmas outfit can also be another way of sharing some holiday time together before Christmas Day.

Christmas History

Take a moment, either during Christmas dinner or after the presents have been opened, to ask everyone to share their favorite memories of Christmases past. Encourage Grandma and Grandpa to tell tales of their childhood and ask younger generations to share some of their favorite Christmas traditions.

Far and Away

Don't forget those family members and friends who can't be with you this Christmas. Make a special part of your Christmas the time when you phone those near and dear to your hearts but far away from your home. Get all the family members to-gether by the phone to sing out Christmas cheer to aunties, uncles, cousins, grandparents, friends, and dear ones.

Something Old, Something Meaningful

Instead of buying gifts, draw names and require each family member to give the person whose name they have drawn something they already own that is meaningful to them, but something they think the other person could use. Make sure that when each gift is presented, the giver tells the story of why they are giving the gift. For example, a favorite aunt could give her college-bound niece the dictionary that she so loved during her own college days, or grandma could give her grandson the book of poems she received from her own grandmother.

A Gift That Can't Be Bought

Instead of giving store-bought gifts, require that everyone only give a gift that can't be bought. A child could give the gift of a car wash to their parent, while a parent could give the gift of cleaning the child's room.

Christmas Story Gifts

A perfect gift exchange for a Christmas party, school class, or Scout troop. Ask everyone to buy an inexpensive gift that would be pleasing to anyone. When all the gift-givers are gath-ered together have them sit in a circle holding their gifts and assign one person the job of reading a favorite Christmas story. While the story is being read, everyone listens carefully. Every time the word ''and'' is used all gifts should be passed to the left. When the story is done you get to open the gift in your hands.

Family Fun

Christmas is a great time to get the family together for some fun games. Break out the cards, the backgammon, chess, or checkers. Play hide-and-seek, board games, or word games. If you are lucky enough to get snow, go outside and make snow angels, build a snowman, ride your sled, or build an igloo. The list of fun is endless but we've included a few family favorites here for your gaming pleasure.

Charades With a Christmas Theme

Instead of the usual movies, book titles, songs or TV shows, use only those with a Christmas theme running through them to keep the holiday spirit going. Here is a refresher course for those of you who don't know how to play Charades.

Here is what you will need:

An egg timer
Pen and paper
Two hats

The object of the game is for a player to act out the title of a movie, book, song, or TV show in the shortest amount of time possible while his team shouts out guesses.

Players should split into two teams. Each team should have at least two players, preferably more. Each team should think of Christmas movies, books, TV shows, or Christmas carols and jot down their titles on the paper. Make sure the other team cannot hear you as you pick your titles. Tear off each title and fold it up and put it in the hat so the other time can't see what it says when they pick it out of the hat. (Note: each team puts their titles in the other team's hat so that teams pick from the titles they don't know.) Now you can start playing.

Player one picks a title out of the hat and must act out the title for his or her team to guess. When player one starts acting the egg timer is turned over. The player cannot use words, and must get the team to guess the answer by acting out actions only. As player one tries to act out the title, the team members shout out their guesses. If someone gets it right before the egg timer is finished, player one's team gets a point.

Here are some hand signals that will help you speed your team's guesses:

A movie: Put one fist in front of one eye and create a little tunnel that you will look through, while squinting with the other. At the same time, pretend you are winding the film of an old-fashioned movie camera with the other hand.

A book: Hold your palms face-up in front you, pinkies together, as if you are reading a book.

A TV show: Draw an imaginary square in the air with your finger.

One finger held up means first word. When you are acting out the first word of your title, hold up one finger. When you are acting out the second, hold up two, etc.

Number of syllables: To illustrate the number of syllables in a word, hold up your fingers indicating the number of syllables and chop those fingers over the arm of the opposite hand. When someone guesses the number of syllables in the word you are going to act out, then show them which syllable you plan to illustrate first by repeating the syllable gesture.

Sounds like: If you want to act out a word that sounds like another word, indicate *sounds like* by holding a cupped hand to an ear. In other words, you will be acting out a word that sounds like the word in the title.

Length of a word: Show that you are going to act out a little word by holding two fingers together as you would if you were indicating an inch. Show that you are going to act out a long word by holding two hands out, far apart.

Be creative and make up other gestures. Here are some good titles to act out. You can come up with many, many more yourselves.

The Grinch Who Stole Christmas
"Silent Night"
"The Twelve Days of Christmas"
A Christmas Story
A Christmas Carol
"Frosty the Snowman"
"Jingle Bells"
Miracle on 34th Street
"Santa Got Run Over by a Reindeer" and so on!

Trivia Games

Take some of the fun facts in this book and make a trivia game out of it. Or if you have a religious background or your kids are in Sunday school, make a trivia game out of bible stories. This is fun for the kids and informative too.

Dictionary Fun

You'll need:

Pen and paper
A dictionary

Break out the dictionary for some fun word games. Pick a game leader. Have the leader pick words out of the dictionary that he or she thinks no one will know the definition of. Write the real definition of each word down on a piece of paper. Read the word aloud and have everyone come up with a definition for it. Each person writes his definition on a scrap of paper and hands it to the leader. The leader reads aloud the word to be defined, then each definition. Players will in turn guess which one they think is the correct definition. If a player guesses the correct definition, that player gets 2 points. If a player guesses someone else's definition, the player who came up with the definition gets 1 point. Play until someone reaches 10 points. It's a fun game, and someone might actually learn something!

Knock Out Whist

A fun card game for the entire family. All you will need is a regular deck of playing cards. Deal out the cards, 7 to each player. Turn the last card over. This is the trump suit.

What is a trump? A trump is a card or suit that will beat any card of another suit that is not a trump suit, regardless of hierarchy. For instance, if hearts are trumps, a three of hearts will beat a king of spades.

Aces are the highest card, kings are next, and so on down to two, which is the lowest card. The player to the left of the dealer leads with a card. Each player in turn throws a card on that card, hoping to be the player with the highest card. You must follow suit if you can. If you cannot, you can trump or throw any card you like. You do not have to trump if you don't want to, unless a trump is led first and then you must follow suit. The first card thrown decides the suit to be followed in that round. The player with the highest card, or the player who trumps in, gets to take the trick. (You cannot trump in if you can follow suit.) The player who takes the trick then leads with the next card until all of the cards are out. The player with the most tricks gets to call trumps in the next round. In the next round, you deal 6 cards to each player. If a player did not get a trick in the previous hand he or she is now out of the game. That's why it's called Knock Out Whist! The game continues as long as there are players to play, next going to 5 cards each, then 4 cards, then 3 cards, etc. If you get in a situation where 2 players have an equal number of tricks at the end of a hand, those players can cut the deck to see who gets to call trump in the next hand. The highest card in the trump suit wins.

Our Family Traditions and Memories

Whether you have special traditions of your own you'd like to write down, or Christmas memories you'd like to share with generations to come, this is a great spot to fill those ideas in and record them forever.

TRADITION/MEMORY _____

RECORDER _____

_____

_____

_____

_____

_____

_____

_____

_____

_____

_____

_____

_____

_____

TRADITION/MEMORY _____

RECORDER _____

_____

_____

_____

_____

_____

_____

_____

_____

_____

_____

_____

_____

_____

_____

_____

_____

TRADITION/MEMORY _____

RECORDER _____

_____

_____

_____

_____

_____

_____

_____

_____

_____

_____

_____

_____

_____

_____

_____

_____

TRADITION/MEMORY _____

RECORDER _____

_____
_____
_____
_____
_____
_____
_____
_____
_____
_____
_____
_____
_____
_____

❧

TRADITION/MEMORY _____

RECORDER _____

_____
_____
_____
_____
_____
_____
_____
_____
_____
_____
_____
_____
_____
_____

TRADITION/MEMORY _____

RECORDER _____

_____

_____

_____

_____

_____

_____

_____

_____

_____

_____

_____

_____

_____

_____

_____

❦

TRADITION/MEMORY _____

RECORDER _____

_____

_____

_____

_____

_____

_____

_____

_____

_____

_____

_____

_____

_____

_____

TRADITION/MEMORY _____

RECORDER _____

_____
_____
_____
_____
_____
_____
_____
_____
_____
_____
_____
_____
_____
_____
_____

❄

TRADITION/MEMORY _____

RECORDER _____

_____
_____
_____
_____
_____
_____
_____
_____
_____
_____
_____
_____
_____
_____
_____
_____

7

Christmas Fun Facts

A little nonsense now and then is relished by the wisest men.
—Roald Dahl

From the exchange of gifts to Santa Claus and his reindeer, Christmas is a wonderful worldwide holiday filled with terrific facts and trivia. Use this chapter to invent your own version of Christmas Jeopardy or as a way to stimulate conversation during dinner. After all, do you know how many towns in the United States are named after Santa Claus?

Religious Facts

Jesus of Nazereth was actually born four to eight years before he is said to be born. His birth occurred during the reign of Herod, who died in 4 B.C., four years "before Christ." In 534 A.D., the man who calculated the year of Jesus's birth made a mistake—a mistake we still live with.

In 1752, the switch was made from the Julian to the Gregorian calendar. When the change was made, eleven days were dropped from the year, moving December 25 eleven days backward. Some Christian sects, called old calendarists, still celebrate Christmas on January 7 (previously December 25 of the Julian calendar).

Traditionally, Christmas was a movable feast celebrated many different times during the year. The choice of December 25 was made by Pope Julius I in the fourth century A.D. because it coincided with the pagan rituals of Winter Solstice, or Return of the Sun. The intent was to replace the pagan celebration with the Christian one.

The Twelve Days of Christmas represent the length of time it took the three wise men to reach the manger of Jesus Christ after his birth. Their arrival on the twelfth day was celebrated in the form of the Feast of Epiphany in medieval France, and later in other countries.

Carols, Stories, and Movies

Max Von Sydow plays Jesus Christ in *The Greatest Story Ever Told* and Satan in *Needful Things*, the only actor to play both parts.

The popular Christmas carol, "The Twelve Days of Christmas" was originally written to help Catholic children in England remember different articles of faith during persecution by Protestant monarchs. The "true love" represented God, and the gifts were all different ideas. The "Partridge in a pear tree," for example, was Christ.

In the Christmas carol "The Twelve Days of Christmas," the total number of gifts that "my true love gave to me" is 364.

In the movie *How the Grinch Stole Christmas*, the Grinch cuts a Santa beard out of felt, but never wears it.

In *A Christmas Carol*, Charles Dickens's initial choice for Scrooge's statement "Bah! Humbug!" was "Bah! Christmas!"

"Jingle Bells" was composed in 1857 by James Pierpont, and was originally called "One Horse Open Sleigh."

"Silent Night" was first played on a guitar. It was sung as part of a church service in Austria and a guitar was used because the church organ was so badly rusted it couldn't be played.

"White Christmas" by Bing Crosby is the greatest-selling Christmas song of all time, selling more than thirty million copies.

Besides Rudolph, the names of Santa's reindeer are Dancer, Dasher, Prancer, Vixen, Comet, Cupid, Donder, and Blitzen.

The lovable Sesame Street characters Bert and Ernie were named in honor of Bert the cop and Ernie the cab driver in *It's a Wonderful Life*.

Trees, Food, and More

The most common flower used in Christmas decorations is the poinsettia.

No reindeer actually live in the North Pole, although there are plenty in Finland.

Christmas tree angels were introduced in the 1850s.

Christmas wreaths are a sign of welcome and long life to all who enter.

Most artificial Christmas trees are manufactured in Korea, Taiwan, or Hong Kong.

The first postage stamp to commemorate Christmas was issued in Austria in 1937.

Since 1991, the sales of artificial Christmas trees have been greater than the sales of live trees.

During December in the Middle Ages, trees were hung with red apples as a symbol of the feast of Adam and Eve, and called Paradise Trees.

Christmas Crackers were invented in 1846 by Tom Smith. He got the idea from the French tradition of wrapping sugared almonds in twists of paper as gifts.

The Canadian province of Nova Scotia leads the world in exporting Christmas trees.

Thomas Edison introduced the first Christmas lights on December 22, 1882.

Carl Otis invented BubbleLights in 1945.

Thomas Nast was the first artist to draw Santa Claus as a fat, jolly, white-whiskered old man.

Until World War I, Lauscha, Germany, supplied virtually all the world's blown-glass Christmas tree ornaments.

The first preprinted Christmas cards were introduced in England in 1843 and designed by London artist John Calcott Horsley. Before that, people used to write their own Christmas greetings.

Many parts of your Christmas tree can actually be eaten. The needles are a good source of Vitamin C and can be used to make tea and spaghetti. And of course, you can buy pine nuts at almost any grocery store.

The abbreviation "Xmas" started with the Greeks. X is the first letter in the Greek word for Christ, Xristos. Therefore, saying Xmas is really saying C-mas.

Kissing under the mistletoe is a tradition that dates back to seventeenth-century England.

The top Christmas tree-producing states are Oregon, Michigan, Wisconsin, Pennsylvania, California, and North Carolina.

The top-selling Christmas trees are balsam fir, douglas fir, fraser fir, noble fir, scotch pine, virginia pine, and white pine.

For every real Christmas tree harvested, two to three seedlings are planted in its place.

In 1914, World War I had just started and was already proving to be one of history's bloodiest wars, but in a surprising act of true Christmas spirit, soldiers fighting in the southern portion of France, Ypres Salient, agreed to temporarily set aside their weapons in honor of a great holiday.

The word "Christmas" means "Mass of Christ," later shortened to "Christ-Mass."

Father Christmas or Santa Claus is based on Saint Nicholas (270–310 A.D.), the patron saint of children.

There are thirty-four places in the United States named "Reindeer." Twenty-seven are located in Alaska.

Facts Around the Globe

In Japan, Christmas Eve is celebrated by eating fried chicken and strawberry shortcake.

It was Queen Victoria's husband, Prince Albert, who brought the first Christmas tree to Windsor Castle in 1834.

In Italy, a naughty child can expect to receive a lump of coal in his stocking.

In the middle of each November, the Christmas lights in Regent Street, London, are traditionally switched on by a celebrity. To be invited to light the lights usually means you are a recent pop favorite.

In Italy, Christmas isn't traditionally celebrated with a Christmas tree. Instead, Italians decorate with small pyramid-shaped wooden stands of fruit.

In Caracas, the capital city of Venezuela, it is customary for the streets to be blocked off on Christmas Eve so that people can roller-skate to church.

In Peru, every Christmas is celebrated with the festive "Great Bullfight."

A common Christmas decoration in Sweden is the Juldukk, a small figurine of a goat. It is usually made of straw. The Jul-bukk is often placed under the tree to protect the gifts.

In Holland, children celebrate Christmas by waiting for the eight-footed horse. Children fill their shoes with hay for the horse and the horse leaves gifts for good children and spanking switches for bad children.

The decorations in London's Trafalgar Square include a large Christmas tree, an annual gift from Oslo, Norway.

United States Trivia

Franklin Pierce was the first president to decorate an official White House Christmas tree.

In 1923, President Calvin Coolidge started the National Christmas Tree Lighting Ceremony now held every year on the White House lawn.

The first official U.S. Christmas stamp was issued in 1962.

Alabama was the first state to recognize Christmas as an official holiday, in 1836.

There are 140 places in the United States with the word "Christmas" in their name, including Merry Christmas Creek, Alaska; Christmas Gift Mine in Pinal County, Arizona; and Merrie Christmas Park in Miami-Dade County, Florida.

There are eleven U.S. towns called "Santa Claus" in eight U.S. states: Alaska, Arizona, Georgia, Indiana, Minnesota, Nevada, Oregon, and Utah.

If Noel is your thing, there are fifty places in the United States with the word "Noel" in their name, including communities named Noel in Colorado, Missouri, and Virginia and Noel Lake in Indiana, near the community of Santa Claus.

The state of California has issued six driver's licenses to Jesus Christ.

Pilgrims forbade the singing of Christmas carols.

Christmas Seals were first sold in the United States in 1907 in Wilmington, Delaware.

The first Christmas tree farm planted in the United States was in 1901 near Trenton, New Jersey.

In the United States alone, more than 2 billion Christmas cards are sent each year.

In 1828, the poinsettia was introduced to the United States from Mexico by Dr. Joel Poinsett, the First U.S. ambassador to Mexico. The flower was renamed in Poinsett's honor.

According to Pennsylvania Dutch tradition, the brother of Santa Claus, Bells Nichols, visits homes on New Year's Eve after children are asleep. The children leave out plates for Santa's brother to fill with cakes and cookies.

President Lyndon B. Johnson's daughter was engaged on Christmas Eve, 1965.

Contrary to popular belief, the day after Thanksgiving is not the busiest shopping day of the year. The two busiest days are actually the Friday and Saturday right before Christmas.

The item most purchased for Christmas is clothing.

Most malls begin decorating for Christmas by October 15.

In 1851, Mark Carr hauled two sleds loaded with trees from the Catskills to the streets of New York and opened the first retail tree lot in the United States.

Merry Christmas and Happy New Year in Many Languages

Use this fun list as a starting point to learning a new language, or have everyone in the family learn how to say Merry Christmas and Happy New Year from those countries where your family originated from.

Afrikaans (South Africa)	*Geseende Kersfees en 'n gelukkige nuwe jaar*
Albanian	*Gëzuar Krishlindjet Vitin e Ri*
Armenian	*Shenoraavor Nor Dari yev Pari Gaghand*
Bura (Nigeria)	*Usa ma ka Kirisimassu* (Merry Christmas)
Czech	*Prejeme van Veselé Vánoce a Stastny Novy Rok*
Danish	*Glædelig Jul og godt nytår!*
Dutch	*Vroliijk Kerstfeest en een Gelukkig Nieuwjaar*
English	Merry Christmas! Happy New Year!
Estonian	*Rõõmsaid Jõulupühi Hääd uut aastat*
Finnish	*Hyvää joulua! Onnellista uutta vuotta!*
French	*Joyeux Noël et Bonne Année*
Gaelic	*Nollaig ShonaBlian nua faoi mhaise duit*
German	*Frohliche Weihnachten und Ein glückliches neues Jahr!*
Greenlandic	*Juullimi pilluaritsi Ukiortaami pilluaritsi*
Hungarian	*Kellemes karácsonyi ünnepeket Boldog új évet*
Icelandic	*Gledileg Jol og Parsaeldt Komandi ar*
Italian	*Buon Natale e Felice Anno Nuovo*
Latin	*Natale hilare et Annun Nuovo*
Latvian	*Prieci'gus Ziemsve'tkus un Laimigu Jauno gadu!*
Lithuanian	*Linksmu Kaledu ir laimi'gu Nauju Metu*
Luxemburgian	*Déi bescht Wënsch!*

Macedonian	*Srekna Bozhik*
Norwegian	*God Jul og Godt NyttÅr*
Polish	*Wesolych Swiat Bozego Narodzenia*
Portuguese	*Feliz Natal e Feliz Ano Novo!*
Romanian	*Sarbatori Fericite La Multi Ani*
Russian	*Pozdravlyau s przdnikom Rozhdestva i c Novym Godom*
Slovak	*Veselé Vianoce A staslivy Novy Rok*
Spanish	*Feliz Navidad y Feliz Año Nuevo*
Swedish	*God Jul och Gott Nytt År*
Ukrainian	*Khristos Razhdaetsya Z Novim Rokom*
Welsh	*Nadolig Llawen a Blwyddyn Newydd Dda*

On This Christmas Day

Besides Jesus, the following people can also claim December 25 as their birthday:

Sir Isaac Newton, physicist/mathematician/astronomer (1642)

Giovanni Battista Somis, composer (1686)

Jacobus Houbraken Dutch, engraver/illustrator (1698)

Pius VI [Giovanni A Braschi] Italy, Pope—1775–99 (1717)

John "Christmas" Beckwith, composer (1750)

Claude Chappe, French engineer and inventor of the optical telegraph (1763)

Clara Harlowe Barton, nurse and founder of the American Red Cross (1821)

E Fernández Arbós, Spanish violinist/conductor/composer (1863)

Eugenie Besserer, actress from *Jazz Singer* (1868)

Quaid-i-Azam Mohammed Ali Jinnah Karachi, who founded Pakistan (1876)

W Starling Burgess, yacht designer of the America Cup's Enterprise (1878)

Joseph V. McCarthy, baseball manager of the New York Yankees (1881)

Maurice Utrillo, painter (1883)

Conrad Hilton, hotel mogul (1887)

Ropert L. Ripley, *Ripley's Believe It or Not* (1893)

Bert Bertram, actor (1893)

Theo Swagemakers, Dutch portrait painter (1898)

Humphrey Bogart, actor (1899)

Raphael Soyer, artist (1899)

Clark M. Clifford, U.S. Secretary of Defense (1906)

Frank Ferguson, actor (1908)

Willian Noel Moffat, architect (1912)

Anwar el-Sadat, Egyptian President (1918)
Eddie Safranski, Pittsburgh, orchestra leader (1918)
Henry Charnock, oceanographer (1920)
Nellie Fox, White Sox infielder (1927)
Bob Martinez, governor of Florida (1934)
Giancarlo Baghetti, racing driver/journalist (1934)
O'Kelly Isley, singer (1937)
François Durr France, tennis player (1942)
Rick Berman, producer (1944)
Gary Sandy, actor (1945)
Noel Redding, rocker (1945)
Ken "The Snake" Stabler, NFL quarterback (1945)
Jimmy Buffett, singer/songwriter (1946)
Larry Csonka, NFL running back (1946)
Connie Petracek, swimmer (1947)
Barbara Mandrell, singer/TV host (1948)
Sissy Spacek, actress (1949)
Arnella Flynn, Errol Flynn's daughter (1953)
Annie Lennox, singer (1954)
Robin Campbell, British reggae vocalist/guitarist (1954)
Shane McGowan, rock vocalist (1957)
Joop Hiele, soccer player (1958)
Rickey Henderson, baseball player (1958)
Michael P. Anderson, Major USAF/astronaut (1959)
Amy Grant, singer (1960)
Dmitri Mironov, NHL defenseman (1965)
Helena Christensen, model/actress (1968)
Jim Dowd Brick, NHL center (1968)
Bernhard Jr., Prince of Netherlands (1969)
Noel Hogan, musician (1971)
Yazmin Fiallos, Miss Universe-Honduras (1976)

Christmas Timeline

Here are some of the greatest moments in Christmas history:

352 First Christmas celebration.

1223 St. Francis of Assisi assembles first Nativity scene in Greccio, Italy.

1510 A decorated Christmas tree recorded at Riga, Latvia.

1610 Tinsel invented in Germany.

1621 Governor William Bradford of Plymouth forbids game playing on Christmas Day.

1651 Massachusetts General Court ordered a fine (five shillings) for "observing any such day as Christmas."

1660 Record of a tree lit with candles in Germany.

1773 Santa Claus started appearing in the American press as "St. A Claus."

1800 Tree ornaments being manufactured in Europe.

1818 First U.S. performance of Handel's *Messiah* in Boston.

1818 First known Christmas carol ("Silent Night, Holy Night" by Franz Joseph Gruber & Joseph Mohr) is sung in Austria.

1819 Popular sketch by Krimmel released depicting an American family with a Christmas tree on the table.

1822 German merchants living in England have decorated trees in their homes.

1823 Clement Moore, an American, writes *A Visit From Saint Nicholas* for his family (now known as *'Twas the Night Before Christmas*).

1831 Louisiana and Arkansas are the first states to observe Christmas as a holiday.

1833 Red poinsettias sold in Philadelphia.

1841 Christmas crackers being manufactured in England.

1843 Charles Dickens writes *A Christmas Carol*.

1843 First commercial Christmas card published.

1846 *London News* publishes a picture of the Royal Family gathered around a Christmas tree. The picture helps popularize the table-top Christmas tree.

1848 *'Twas the Night Before Christmas* published.

1880 Illustrator Thomas Nast introduced a rotund Santa for Christmas issues of *Harper's* magazine.

1880 German glass ornaments sold in Woolworth's.

1882 First electric Christmas tree lights sold in New York.

1892 Wire hook for hanging tree ornaments is patented in the United States.

1895 The first electrically lighted Christmas tree was displayed in the White House.

1896 The T. Eaton Company produces its first Christmas catalogue.

1905 Santa Claus arrives by wagon at the T. Eaton Company store in Toronto.

1907 The first Christmas Seal was issued to help fight tuberculosis.

1917 J. C. Hall (of Hallmark) imported fancy decorated envelope linings from France to sell as "gift dressing."

1923 Pink poinsettias produced.

1931 Santa Claus was shown not as an elf, but as human size in a series of illustrations for Coca-Cola advertisements introduced in 1931.

1932 The song "Santa Claus Is Coming to Town" was written.

1939 Rudolph the Red-Nosed Reindeer was created by Robert May for Montgomery Ward department store as a Christmas promotion.

1947 The song "Here Comes Santa Claus" was written.

1947 The film *Miracle on 34th Street* was released.

1958 Alan Freed's Christmas Rock & Roll Spectacular opens.

1959 Richard Starkey [Ringo Starr] receives his first drum set as a Christmas gift.

2000 The total cost of all 364 gifts mentioned in the song "The Twelve days of Christmas" is $60,307.18 (or $93,187.66, if purchased on the Internet).

Resources

Web Resources

An Online Christmas Songbook
http://rememberjosie.org/carols/index.asp

This terrific site by Christopher R. Baker offers over 100 Christmas carols—words and music. Perfect for a caroling party, just print out enough copies for everyone. And if you don't read music, you can listen to it right through your computer and sing along. One of the best Christmas sites on the Web.

Santa Claus at Claus.com
http://www.claus.com

"The merriest place in cyberspace" has everything every kid needs to keep up on North Pole happenings. Check your naughty or nice rating, choose an Elf buddy, play games, sing along with all new Christmas songs, check out the recipes, and most importantly—follow Santa's sleigh on Christmas Eve.

The Annual Nord Tracks Santa
http://www.noradsanta.org

Probably the best Santa tracking Web site, this stunning site also offers songs and a Santa history.

Christmas Central
http://rats2u.com/christmas/christmas_index.htm

Links to almost everything Christmas. This site is a guide to Christmas animations for your computer, clip art, crafts, virtual cards, music, recipes, and much more.

Have Yourself a Merry Little Christmas Page
http://www.kate.net/holidays/christmas/world.html

Among other things, this terrific page gives you an idea of how Christmas is celebrated in almost twenty countries.

Childfun.com Christmas
http://childfun.com/christmas

One of the Internet's premier parenting Web site presents all sorts of ideas and projects for Christmas, all geared to kids. Whether it's cooking, crafts, or games, this site has ideas to keep the kids busy for days.

A Christmastime Celebration
http://www.myholidayplace.com/christmas/home.html

Finally, a page that understands the true meaning of Christmas. Not only will you find the story of Christmas here, but also some of our most celebrated Christmas stories—from Scrooge to the Grinch. Also humor, stories, and gift ideas. A great page for the entire family.

New York Institute of Photography Tips on Taking Photos of Holiday Lights
http://www.nyip.com/tips/topic_holidaylights1298.html

A page dedicated to teaching amateurs how to ensure terrific holiday pictures.

Books for the Entire Family

Twas the Night Before Christmas by Clement C. Moore

This classic poem where the "children were nestled all snug in their beds" is essential for every Christmas bookshelf. Available in hardcover, paperback, and even pop-up versions. You're bound to find a copy that everyone will love.

A Christmas Carol by Charles Dickens

This quintessential Christmas story has been in publication since 1843 and deserves to be owned in both book form and on video or DVD.

How the Grinch Stole Christmas by Dr. Seuss

For over fifty years Dr. Seuss's small-hearted Grinch has ranked right up there with Scrooge when it comes to being the crankiest holiday grump.

Books for Children

Rudolph the Red-Nosed Reindeer by Robert Lewis May

Created in 1939 as part of a giveaway from the Montgomery Ward department store, Rudolph has become the best-known and best-loved reindeer in all of Santa's herd.

The Polar Express by Chris Van Allsburg (Illustrator)

This delightful tale of a young boy lying awake on Christmas Eve to see Santa Claus sweep by and take him on a trip with other children to the North Pole is guaranteed to become a Christmas classic.

The Berenstain Bears Christmas and *The Berenstein Bears Christmas Tree* by Stan and Jan Berenstain

It's Christmastime in Bear Country and the entire Bernstein family is on hand to delight children and adults with their antics.

A Little House Christmas: Holiday Stories from the Little House Books by Laura Ingalls Wilder

A collection of stories from some of Ingalls's most popular books have been reprinted in this special holiday volume.

Nine Days to Christmas by Marie Hall Ets

A little girl's first *posada* (Mexican Christmas festival) will make Mexico come alive for all children.

Babar and Father Christmas by Jean de Brunhoff

Everyone's favorite elephant king travels to the North Pole to find Father Christmas.

Christmas in Noisy Village by Astrid Lindgren

A charming story about the children of Noisy Village and how they celebrate Christmas.

Jan Brett's Christmas Treasury by Jan Brett

Celebrate the magic of Christmas with this giant treasury of Jan Brett's best-loved books. This collection includes seven of Brett's classics: *The Mitten, The Wild Christmas Reindeer, Trouble with Trolls, The Twelve Days of Christmas, The Hat, Christmas Trolls,* and *The Night Before Christmas*.

Olive, the Other Reindeer by Vivian Walsh, J. Otto Seibold

Olive is a dog who, upon hearing "Rudolph the Red-Nosed Reindeer,'' feels that she's received her calling. Deciding she must be a reindeer, she heads to the North Pole to see if she can join Santa's reindeer team.

Books for Adults and Gifts

A Cup of Christmas Tea by Tom Hegg and Warren Hanson

The true meaning of Christmas is brought to life in this heartwarming poem. In the midst of the Christmas rush, a man decides to go visit his sick great-aunt. While he's there, peace, love, and Christmas spirit surround the two as they share a cup of Christmas tea.

Silent Night: The Remarkable 1914 Christmas Truce by Stanley Weintraub

A wonderfully uplifting story about one of the greatest ironies in history. A few days before the first Christmas of World War I, hundreds of cold, trench-bound combatants put aside their arms and, in defiance of their orders, tacitly agreed to stop the killing in honor of the holiday.

Craft and Recipe Books

Christmastime Treats: Recipes and Crafts for the Whole Family by Sara Perry

An array of recipes and craft projects for the whole family. Includes great decoration ideas, wonderful recipes, and even menus everyone will love.

Martha Stewart's Christmas Parties and Projects for the Holidays
Martha Stewart's Christmas
Handmade Christmas, Decorating for the Holidays
Crafts and Keepsakes for the Holidays
Christmas with Martha Stewart Living
All by Martha Stewart. Essential books for every Martha fan.

Gingerbread Houses: A Complete Guide to Baking, Building, and Decorating by Christa Currie

The gingerbread house guide will help anyone, whether or not you are an expert baker or architect, build the gingerbread house of your dreams.

Baking for Christmas: 50 of the Best Cookie, Bread and Cake Recipes for Holiday Gift Giving, Decorating and Eating by Maria Polushkin, Maria Robbins

A collection of fifty holiday baking recipes.

Joy of Cooking Christmas Cookies by Irma S. Rombauer

A collection of over a hundred recipes, old classics and brand new extras, from cooking's greatest cookbook author.

Christmas from the Heart of the Home by Susan Branch

Mouth-watering recipes, decorating tips, and simple crafts all done with the warmth and charm of Susan Branch.

Mary Engelbreit's Christmas Companion: The Mary Engelbreit Look and How to Get It by Mary Engelbreit

A Mary Engelbreit home-decorating collection that captures the magic of Christmas.

Holiday Movies for the Entire Family

It's a Wonderful Life (1946)
Starring James Stewart, Donna Reed

This American classic is sure to warm even the biggest Scrooge. Watch as George Bailey's guardian angel shows George what the world would be like if he had never existed, giving us all an idea of how important even the smallest person is.

A Christmas Carol (1951)
Starring Kathleen Harrison, Alastair Sim

One of the many movies based on the Charles Dickens classic. Miser Ebenezer Scrooge learns the true meaning of Christmas and re-forms his heartless and money-grubbing ways after being visited on Christmas Eve by four ghosts—his old business partner Jacob Marley, the Ghost of Christmas Past, the Ghost of Christmas Present, and the Ghost of Christmas Yet to Come.

White Christmas (1954)
Starring Bing Crosby, Danny Kaye, Rosemary Clooney, Vera-Ellen

Two of the most talented song-and-dance men team up after the war to become one of the hottest acts in show business. A veritable treasury of Irving Berlin classics will keep your toes tapping and your heart soaring.

Miracle on 34th Street (1947)
Starring Maureen O'Hara, John Payne, Edmund Gwenn, Natalie Wood

When the real Santa Claus is hired to play himself at a New York City department store, his gentle spirit and magical powers soon transform those around him, including a little girl and her world-weary mother.

Frosty the Snowman (1969)
Narrated by Jimmy Durante

When a magical hat is placed upon Frosty's head, the hapless snowman is brought to life and must face a series of adventures and try to keep away from the evil magician before he can find safety and happiness at the North Pole.

A Charlie Brown Christmas (1965)
Featuring the Peanuts Gang

A true classic, and essential viewing for everyone! While searching for the true meaning of Christmas, Charlie Brown finds it in a tiny Christmas tree and the love of friends.

Rudolph the Red-Nosed Reindeer (1964)
Narrated by Burl Ives

The North Pole's favorite reindeer saves Christmas when a big storm threatens to keep Santa indoors.

The Little Drummer Boy (1968)
Starring Jose Ferrer, Greer Garson

In this animated classic, a lonely little boy discovers the greatest gift of all when he visits a manger in Bethlehem.

How the Grinch Stole Christmas (1966)
Directed by Chuck Jones
Narrated by Boris Karloff
By Dr. Seuss

The animated tale of the Grinch and Cindy Lou Who.

Jingle All the Way (1996)
Starring Arnold Schwarzenegger, Sinbad, Phil Hartman
   This fun comedy is about two fathers trying to locate and pur-
chase the same hugely popular action toy on Christmas Eve.

National Lampoon's Christmas Vacation (1989)
Starring Chevy Chase, Beverly D'Angelo, Randy Quaid
   Clark and Ellen Griswald prepare for a quiet Christmas with the
kids, when their home is invaded by all their crazy and assorted rela-
tives.

A Christmas Story (1984)
Starring Darren McGavin, Peter Billingsley
   A wonderfully comic nostalgic look at Christmas in the 1940s.

Gift Ideas That Give

Give a gift to yourself or a friend and help others by donating your time or money to some of these fantastic organizations. The perfect solution for that person who has everything.

Besides the organizations listed below, also consider contributing to your local animal shelters, churches, Red Cross, arts programs, or clubs for children.

Alzheimer's Association
919 North Michigan Avenue, Suite 1100
Chicago, Illinois 60611–1676
http://www.alz.org
The Alzheimer's Association is the largest national voluntary health organization committed to finding a cure for Alzheimer's and helping those affected by the disease.

American Heart Association
7272 Greenville Avenue
Dallas, TX 75231
http://www.AmericanHeart.org
The American Heart Association is a national voluntary health agency whose mission is to reduce disability and death from cardio-vascular diseases and stroke.

American Parkinson Disease Association, Inc.
1250 Hylan Boulevard, Suite 4B
Staten Island, NY 10305
www.apdaparkinson.org
Dedicated to funding Parkinson's research, providing comprehensive medical information, extensive public/professional education and support services. 65 chapters, 58 centers, 226 affiliated support groups.

American Red Cross
P.O. Box 37243
Washington, DC 20013
http://www.redcross.org

This diverse organization serves humanity and helps you by providing relief to victims of disaster, both locally and globally. The Red Cross is responsible for half of the nation's blood supply and blood products.

ASPCA
424 East 92nd Street
New York, NY 10128
http://www.aspca.org

The American Society for the Prevention of Cruelty to Animals exists to promote humane principles, prevent cruelty, and alleviate fear, pain, and suffering in animals.

A Child's Hope Fund
2532 Abedul Street
Carlsbad, CA 92009
www.achildshopefund.org

Fight pediatric cancer, diabetes, and hunger through medical and food programs, health education, and emotional/spiritual support for children in nine countries endangered by disease, poverty, war, and natural disaster.

Doctors Without Borders
Call 1–888–392–0392, 24 hours a day, 7 days a week
P.O. Box 2247
New York, NY 10116–2247
http://www.doctorswithoutborders.org/donate

Doctors Without Borders supports global medical relief missions.

Farm Sanctuary
Farm Sanctuary—East
P.O. Box 150
Watkins Glen, NY 14891
Phone: 607–583–2225
Fax: 607–583–2041

Farm Sanctuary—West
P.O. Box 1065
Orland, CA 95963
Phone: 530–865–4617
Fax: 530–865–4622

Since incorporating in 1986, Farm Sanctuary has established America's premier farm animal shelters and waged effective campaigns to stop farm animal cruelty.

The Heifer Project
1015 Louisiana Street
Little Rock, AR 72202
http://www.heifer.org

Give the gift of a heifer, water buffalo, llama, goat, sheep, pig, trees, rabbits, bees, chicks, ducks, or geese. Your donation will give such a gift to a needy family.

Make-A-Wish
3550 North Central Avenue, Suite 300
Phoenix, AZ 85012–2127
http://www.makeawish.org

The Make-A-Wish Foundation grants the wishes of children with life-threatening illnesses to enrich the human experience with hope, strength, and joy.

National Breast Cancer Foundation, Inc.
16633 N. Dallas Parkway, Suite 600
Addison, TX 75001
www.nationalbreastcancer.org

Educates women on life-saving techniques of early detection of breast cancer; provides support for breast cancer patients; free-to-low-cost mammography for underserved women.

National Center for Missing and Exploited Children
699 Prince Street
Alexandria, VA 22314
www.missingkids.com

Spearheads national and international efforts to locate and recover missing children and raises public awareness about ways to prevent child abduction, molestation, and sexual exploitation.

National Coalition Against Domestic Violence
P.O. Box 18749
Denver, CO 80218
www.ncadv.org

Represents a national network of local programs working to eliminate domestic violence. Provides information and referrals, access to free plastic surgery and cosmetic dentistry to victims, and community awareness campaigns.

National Park Foundation
1101 17th Street NW, Suite 1102
Washington, DC 20036
www.nationalparks.org

Honors, enriches, and expands the legacy of private philanthropy that helped create and continues to sustain America's national parks through competitive grants and direct support.

National Wildlife Federation
11100 Wildlife Center Drive
Reston, VA 20190
www.nwf.org

Saving wildlife and wild places with citizen action and educational outreach, including publications like *Ranger Rick*. Giving people knowledge and tools to make a difference.

The Nature Conservancy
4245 North Fairfax Drive
Arlington, VA 22307
www.nature.org

Buys and protects land to save our world's rare plants and animals from extinction. Over 12 million acres protected—rain forests, prairies, wetlands, and beaches.

Pediatric AIDS Foundation
2950 31st Street, Suite 125
Santa Monica, CA 90405
www.pedaids.org

Daily 1,600 children worldwide are newly infected with HIV. The Pediatric AIDS Foundation creates hope for children with HIV/AIDS and other life-threatening diseases through research, training, and advocacy programs.

Salvation Army

http://www.salvationarmy.org

Internationally the Salvation Army works in just over 100 countries using more than 140 languages. There are over 14,000 Corps (worship centers) as well as a wide range of social, medical, educational, and other community services.

The Salvation Army has branches all over the world and is separated into four terrorities in the United States. Check out their Web site for the branch closest to you.

The September 11 Fund

c/o United Way of New York City

2 Park Avenue

New York, NY 10016

http://www.uwnyc.org/sep11

Established by United Way of New York City and the New York Community Trust to meet the needs of victims, families, and communities affected by the terrorist attack of September 11.

SIDS Educational Services, Inc.

2905 64th Avenue

Cheverly, MD 20785

www.sidssurvivalguide.org;www.dancingonthemoon.org

Provides free information, referrals, and peer counseling on Sudden Infant Death Syndrome to families and professionals.

Twin Towers Fund

General Post Office

P.O. Box 26999

New York, NY 10087-6999

http://twintowersfund.vista.com

Assists, supports, and recognizes the families of the members of the uniformed services of the New York City Fire Department and its Emergency Medical Service Command, the New York City Police Department, the Port Authority of New York and New Jersey, the New York State Office of Court Administration, and other government offices who lost their lives or were injured by the terrorist attacks of September 11.

Your Christmas Lists

A Wish List

Wishes are wonderful things. Take the time to sit down each year and write out a wish list of everything you'd love to have. Don't limit yourself to material items, but wish for immaterial things as well: good health, a great haircut, peace for people everywhere. Wish for others: a new baby for your brother, a wonderful boyfriend for your sister, an exotic trip for your mom, spiritual peace for your spouse. A perfect day for your dog . . . Let your mind go and just dream for yourself and for those you love. Dream for those you don't even know. Wishing can change your attitude for the day and put you in a wonderful, generous, peaceful frame of mind. Keep a journal of your wishes from year to year and look back at previous years' wishes to see how you and your family have changed!

TODAY I WISH . . .   YEAR _____

_____

_____

_____

_____

_____

_____

_____

_____

_____

_____

_____

_____

_____

TODAY I WISH . . .   YEAR _____

_____

_____

_____

_____

_____

_____

_____

_____

_____

_____

_____

_____

_____

_____

TODAY I WISH . . .   YEAR _____

_____

_____

_____

_____

_____

_____

_____

_____

_____

_____

_____

_____

_____

_____

TODAY I WISH . . .   YEAR _____

_____
_____
_____
_____
_____
_____
_____
_____
_____
_____
_____
_____
_____
_____
_____

TODAY I WISH . . .   YEAR _____

_____
_____
_____
_____
_____
_____
_____
_____
_____
_____
_____
_____
_____
_____

TODAY I WISH . . . YEAR _____

_____

_____

_____

_____

_____

_____

_____

_____

_____

_____

_____

_____

_____

_____

_____

❧

TODAY I WISH . . . YEAR _____

_____

_____

_____

_____

_____

_____

_____

_____

_____

_____

_____

_____

_____

_____

_____

A Gift List

Giving is our favorite part of the holiday season. We love to find the perfect gift for that special loved one, or make that wonderful gesture that shows how much we care. Sometimes the best gift is an offer to babysit, or a day spent with your loved one. Sometimes a trip to the spa, sometimes a picnic. Be creative with your gift giving and please know that giving is not about a price tag. You can come up with the best gifts of all and not even spend a cent. Read to an older community member, make someone a meal. Sometimes the best gift of all is the gift of your time and yourself.

Make a list each year of gifts you'd like to give and keep a running record over time of what you've given each person in your life. It's a wonderful record of your generosity and the spirit of Christmas.

My Gift List

PERSON	Gift	YEAR

PERSON	Gift	YEAR

PERSON	Gift	YEAR

PERSON	Gift	YEAR

PERSON	Gift	YEAR

PERSON   Gift   YEAR

_____

_____

_____

_____

_____

_____

_____

_____

_____

_____

_____

_____

_____

_____

PERSON   Gift   YEAR

_____

_____

_____

_____

_____

_____

_____

_____

_____

_____

_____

_____

_____

Index